Lead FROM THE Start

How to Succeed as the New Principal of Your School

TOMMY REDDICKS
TINA MERRIWEATHER SEYMOUR

Solution Tree | Press
a division of
Solution Tree

Copyright © 2020 by Solution Tree Press

Materials appearing here are copyrighted. With one exception, all rights are reserved. Readers may reproduce only those pages marked "Reproducible." Otherwise, no part of this book may be reproduced or transmitted in any form or by any means (electronic, photocopying, recording, or otherwise) without prior written permission of the publisher.

555 North Morton Street
Bloomington, IN 47404
800.733.6786 (toll free) / 812.336.7700
FAX: 812.336.7790

email: info@SolutionTree.com
SolutionTree.com

Visit **go.SolutionTree.com/leadership** to download the free reproducibles in this book.

Printed in the United States of America

Library of Congress Cataloging-in-Publication Data

Names: Reddicks, Tommy, author. | Seymour, Tina Merriweather, author.
Title: Lead from the start : how to succeed as the new principal of your
   school / Tommy Reddicks, Tina Merriweather Seymour.
Description: Bloomington, IN : Solution Tree Press, 2020. | Includes
   bibliographical references and index.
Identifiers: LCCN 2019040025 (print) | LCCN 2019040026 (ebook) | ISBN
   9781949539356 (paperback) | ISBN 9781949539363 (ebook)
Subjects: LCSH: School principals--United States. | School
   principals--Professional relationships--United States. | Educational
   leadership--United States. | School management and organization--United
   States. | Teacher-principal relationships--United States.
Classification: LCC LB2831.92 .R39 2020 (print) | LCC LB2831.92 (ebook) |
   DDC 371.2/012--dc23
LC record available at https://lccn.loc.gov/2019040025
LC ebook record available at https://lccn.loc.gov/2019040026

Solution Tree
Jeffrey C. Jones, CEO
Edmund M. Ackerman, President

Solution Tree Press
President and Publisher: Douglas M. Rife
Associate Publisher: Sarah Payne-Mills
Art Director: Rian Anderson
Managing Production Editor: Kendra Slayton
Production Editor: Laurel Hecker
Content Development Specialist: Amy Rubenstein
Copy Editor: Mark Hain
Text Designer: Abigail Bowen
Editorial Assistant: Sarah Ludwig

Acknowledgments

Solution Tree Press would like to thank the following reviewers:

Karen Carstens
Principal
Tritt Elementary School
Marietta, Georgia

Aaron Else
Principal
Hosp Elementary School
Frisco, Texas

Jennifer Evans
Principal
Burnham School
Cicero, Illinois

Nathaniel Provencio
Principal
Minnieville Elementary School
Woodridge, Virginia

Kellie Rapp
Principal
Tadlock Elementary School
Frisco, Texas

Josh Ray
Principal
East Pointe Elementary School
Greenwood, Arkansas

Table of Contents

Reproducible pages are in italics.

About the Authors ix

Introduction 1
    The Challenges of Becoming a Principal. 3
    Preparation for Leadership 7
    How to Use This Book 9

CHAPTER 1
Understand the Setting 13
    What Kind of School Are You Leading? 13
    What Kind of Leader Came Before You?. 16
    What Are You Working With?. 20
    Whom Are You Working With? 23
    Summary 28
    Chapter 1 Reflection Questions 29

CHAPTER 2
Prepare for Opening Day. 31
    Preparing Staff 32
    Preparing the Logistics 34
    Preparing Families. 36
    Preparing for Special Populations 37
    Summary 40
    Chapter 2 Reflection Questions. 43

CHAPTER 3
Build Educational Relationships 45
Emotional Intelligence 46
Relationship Evaluation 49
Fundraising and Friend-Raising 54
Community Engagement 56
Summary 61
Chapter 3 Reflection Questions 62

CHAPTER 4
Manage the Operation 63
Task Delegation 64
Managed Services 70
Emergency Planning and Crisis Management 81
Asset Inventory 81
Summary 82
Chapter 4 Reflection Questions 84

CHAPTER 5
Codify Schoolwide Norms 85
Establishing Norms 85
Codifying Schoolwide and Classroom Procedures 89
Responding Appropriately to Misbehavior 92
Keeping Students on Track Academically 97
Summary 98
Chapter 5 Reflection Questions 99

CHAPTER 6
Develop Academic Systems 101
Academics and Engagement 101
The Case for Codification and Simplification 107
What to Teach: A Guaranteed and Viable Curriculum 113
How to Teach It: Instructional Practices 116
How to Monitor It: Assessment Practices 117
Customization for Students and Communities 117
Summary 126
Chapter 6 Reflection Questions 127

CHAPTER 7
Manage Your Staff 129
   Managing Your Staff as Individuals 129
   Managing Your Staff as a Whole. 130
   Responding to Difficult Situations 140
   Summary 150
   Chapter 7 Reflection Questions. *152*

CHAPTER 8
Administer Your Budget 153
   Budget Boundaries. 153
   Approaches to Planning and Spending. 155
   Rough Calculations. 158
   Federal Grants. 162
   Other Sources of Supplemental Funding 165
   Summary 167
   Chapter 8 Reflection Questions. *168*

Epilogue 169

APPENDIX
Reproducibles. 171
   Initial Walkthrough Checklist 172
   Basic Budget Considerations 175
   Beginning-of-the-Year Preparations Checklist. 177
   Facility Checklist 178
   Vendor and Subcontractor Contact List 181
   Budget Contact List 183
   School Income Template. 184
   School Expenses Template 185
   Federal Funding Programs 186
   Title I Budget Template. 187

References and Resources 189

Index 197

About the Authors

**Tommy Reddicks** is the CEO of Paramount Schools of Excellence in Indianapolis, Indiana. He started Paramount Brookside in 2010 in the Eastside neighborhood, and now oversees a growing network of schools in the same urban area. Reddicks is a former assistant principal at Knowledge Quest Academy in Milliken, Colorado, and served as a curriculum consultant and school music teacher in public, private, and charter schools between 1995 and 2008.

Tommy is a past president of the Indiana Curriculum and Instruction Association, and past president of the Near Eastside Community Organization (NESCO) in Indianapolis. He is a member of the Equity Coalition for the National Center for Special Education in Charter Schools. He has been a featured keynote speaker and trainer in the field of school health, piloting the Paramount Health Data Project since 2012. In 2014, Tommy published *The Insane Riddle, Code, and Secret Math Book*, a collaborative effort with his daughter Madeline featuring two hundred original riddles. In 2017, Tommy was featured on the education news website *The 74* as one of the emerging leaders reinventing America's schools. That same year, Paramount Schools were awarded five-star status by the state of Indiana. In 2018, his flagship K–8 school, Paramount Brookside, was awarded the National Blue Ribbon Schools award. Tommy has also composed and released two musical albums, *Time and Space* and *A New Dimension*.

Tommy graduated from the University of Wyoming with a bachelor's and a master's in music education. He later received his administrative licensure from the University of Phoenix.

**Tina Merriweather Seymour** is a veteran principal and leadership coach who serves as the founder and executive director of Strategic Learning Solutions, LLC, an association of educators that provides educational consulting and professional development to K–16 schools. For seven years, Tina was the principal of Northview Middle School in Indianapolis, Indiana. Under her leadership, Northview became an International Baccalaureate Middle Years Programme World School and was recognized by the National Forum to Accelerate Middle-Grades Reform as a School to Watch, an award given to exemplars in educating adolescents.

Tina's twenty-one years of experience in urban education also include serving as an assistant principal at Ben Davis High School in Indianapolis, the largest and most comprehensive tenth- through twelfth-grade high school in the state. Prior to administration, she began her career in education in 1998 as a middle school language arts teacher at Speedway Junior High School in Speedway, Indiana, and served on the faculty that led the school to becoming an Indiana Four Star School.

Tina currently teaches on the faculty of the College of Education at Butler University in Indianapolis as an adjunct professor for its premier master's program for school administration, the Experiential Program for Preparing School Principals. She is also a facilitator for the Indiana Association of School Principals leadership academy, Indiana New Administrator Leadership Institute.

Tina was born and raised in Indianapolis where she earned a bachelor of arts in secondary education from the University of Indianapolis and a master of science in educational administration from Butler University.

To book Tommy Reddicks or Tina Merriweather Seymour for professional development, contact pd@SolutionTree.com.

Introduction

Being a school principal is hard work. We know. We've done it. We've caught ourselves wondering, "Who in their right minds would want to take on such an endless task? Why subject ourselves to so much stress?" The answer to those questions is easy. Leadership matters. If we think back to what first called us into leadership roles, many of us can say that we went into the field of education with dreams of becoming life-changing teachers like those portrayed in *Stand and Deliver* (Musca & Menéndez, 1988) and *Dead Poets Society* (Haft, Witt, Thomas, & Weir, 1989). After a few years of magical teaching moments that made us feel like masters of the classroom, we wanted to expand our sphere of influence and sought leadership roles that would allow us to have a greater impact on student success. After all, success in the classroom should be replicable to the larger scale of a school, right?

Of course, we quickly learned that the transition to a building leadership role is not quite that simple. We could succeed if only we could get teachers to cooperate and emulate what we had done in our classrooms. If only parents and community members and district administrators would just give us a little time and space to figure out this leadership thing. Unfortunately, the pressures of standardized test scores and state-assigned school ratings don't allow for much grace or time for trial and error. The stakes are higher than ever before in education, and there is no silver bullet for creating and leading the perfect school model. But after more than four decades of combined experience in teaching and school administration, we can tell you there is a focused, strategic pathway for accelerated success that will put you on a trajectory to truly lead from the start.

We can't overstate the importance of effective leadership in education, and the issue is magnified even more considering what's at stake: the lives of our youth. School leadership matters so much that, in summarizing the results of a six-year study, researchers Karen Seashore Louis, Kenneth Leithwood, Kyla Wahlstrom, and Stephen Anderson (2010) state, "We have not found a single case of a school improving its student achievement record in the absence of talented leadership" (p. 9). Amplifying this, *Empirical Economics* highlights a 2017 study saying "a single school looking to improve student academic achievement could simply hire a high-quality principal, or at the very least avoid low-quality principals" (Dhuey & Smith, 2017, p. 852).

Because of leaders' critical influence on learning, consistency and longevity in school leadership are matters of national concern. Many new administrators leave the profession within their first five years at the helm. In fact, in the United States alone, twenty-five thousand principals (a quarter of all principals in the country) leave their schools each year, and 50 percent quit during their third year in the role (School Leaders Network, 2014). With more than a decade of this continual revolving-door exit pattern compounding the problem in the United States, an astounding 60 percent of current school principals have been at their schools less than three years (Taie & Goldring, 2017).

This problem persists globally as well. In addition to world educational rankings that can drive regular calls for change, work-related stress and local politics seem to play universal roles in school-leader turnover. Rotations of boards, municipalities, and political parties often contribute to a destabilization of the school leadership position. In Brazil, for example, "When a new party takes office, there is a sharp increase in the share of schools with a new headmaster the following year" (Akhtari, Moreira, & Trucco, 2017, p. 18). In an attempt to better understand the lack of persistence of quality school leadership in Japan, a 2019 study (Nitta, Deguchi, Iwasaki, Kanchika, & Inoue, 2019) connects high depression and occupational stress in principals and vice principals, citing workload and role ambiguity as major contributors to depression. In the United Kingdom, the 2015 NAHT survey of school recruitment showed that 72 percent of schools struggled to find a suitable head teacher, with 22 percent failing to recruit. These recruitment deficits often force more new leaders into the position rather than relying on the traditional deputy-head matriculation.

With schools annually losing an increasing number of experienced leaders, their replacements are "being thrown into the deep end of the pool without adequate support, impacting schools, teachers, students, and our country" (School Leaders Network, 2014, p. 2). Not only does the principal churn (or continual leader turnover) phenomenon have deep financial implications for schools and their communities, but the academic setbacks from continual changes in leadership have extensive damaging effects on students in the short and long terms:

> As a result of principal churn, students achieve less in both math and reading during the first year after leader turnover, and schools that experience principal churn year-after-year realize serious

cumulative negative effects on students—a condition that is exacerbated for schools serving underprivileged students. (School Leaders Network, 2014, p. 3)

Despite—or perhaps because of—the critical nature of effective, consistent school leadership, being a principal is an extremely difficult job, especially in the first year or two at a school.

The Challenges of Becoming a Principal

To illustrate some common experiences new principals face, we take you on two brief journeys with Maggie Trendel and Trenton Wallace (not their real names), whose stories are emblematic of the challenges of school leadership.

Mighty Maggie

Maggie Trendel was born and raised in San Antonio, Texas. Both of her parents were teachers, and she eagerly followed in their footsteps, landing in an urban school district in the heart of South San Antonio. As her aptitude for education grew and her potential became more apparent, her administrative team urged her to pursue leadership. After two and a half years, she had earned her master's degree in educational leadership along with her principal's license. She was excited—all the great lessons she had learned in the classroom would soon take root in her leadership of other educators and, indirectly, in students. Life was full of opportunity, and she couldn't wait for the next chapter in her career.

After a year of waiting for a position to open in her district, Maggie began to realize that promotion from within might take too long. She was ready *now*. She was licensed and had all but closed the door on teaching in the classroom. So she began broadening her search, applying to jobs in multiple states and to positions in rural schools, community schools, and charter schools, eager to get in the game. Soon the phone began to ring, and three months later, she was the principal of a school two states away. The district's administrative committee had hired her via videoconference, and she could tell the school needed her help. The pay was fantastic, and the opportunity for growth seemed boundless.

When she first walked into her new building, Maggie was humbled. It was a sixty-thousand-square-foot, brown brick structure built in the 1950s, weather worn, and pockmarked with graffiti. The open windows and giant vents seemed to make strange frowning faces to passersby. An hour later, after a quick tour from her new facilities manager, she learned the heating, ventilation, and air-conditioning (HVAC) system was in disrepair, the boiler was a vintage monstrosity that vibrated violently every fifteen minutes, the ceiling in the main office leaked (gushed) with every rain, and the kitchen was no longer serviceable. Still, Maggie was an optimist. She would meet each challenge with a focused attack and a cost-effective outcome.

As the school year began, Maggie found that her inherited teachers were not equipped to meet the challenges that their students presented. Issues with preparedness, rigor, standards alignment, and sensitivity were collapsing any chance at growth and improvement. Curriculum options at the school were outdated, and the poor building conditions were harming the academic environment. The school culture was impossible to navigate, with reactive systems failing to combat erupting problems. Soon, parents who were initially enthusiastic about the leadership change were becoming discouraged. They were getting vocal and making repeated noisy appearances at board meetings. Their new leader was slowly proving to be ineffective.

Maggie was faced with mounting challenges from all angles, and crafted an in-depth presentation to her superintendent, who merely pacified her efforts with pleasantries and goodwill. Still resilient, she pressed on, risking her district reputation by presenting her issues to the school board and proposing options for stimulating her struggling system. She explained that her staff would need a transfer-driven shake-up and additional capacity added to the leadership team. The district board members listened intently and thanked her for her passionate presentation, promising to provide her with a thoughtful response once they had time to discuss the situation. Two weeks later, Maggie received the following carefully crafted message.

Ms. Trendel

CC: Superintendent Chambers

As representatives of this educational organization, we are proud of the responsibility given to us as board members. Our schools serve a large, diverse population in many buildings that may never again see their full potential, all with teachers and support staff who work tirelessly and selflessly in a market that doesn't fairly compare to other professions. These are the conditions within which we hire new leadership, and within which we all seek to make a difference.

As a group convened to act as a guardrail over organizational policy and fiscal matters, we recognize that it is the job of the school leader to manage day-to-day operations amid the myriad of challenges those same operations may present. And, while we admire your tenacity in advocating for your situation, the district is not in a position at this time to make any financial change in building or staffing support. Additionally, the board shares a common concern over the growing feedback from your school parents and the surrounding community regarding school safety and student performance.

As a board, we encourage you to coordinate future concerns with the superintendent, and we thank you for your continued efforts working with our students and their families.

Two years later, Maggie is back in San Antonio, working as a grants management coordinator for the state of Texas. Her former school continues to underperform, presenting the same challenges to the new principal who replaced her.

Pause & Reflect

Which of Maggie's actions were justified, and which actions, however well intended, let her down? Could other approaches have achieved better results?

Trenton's Trials

Trenton Wallace was a rising star as an assistant principal in a rural charter school in Ohio. He had cofounded the school with the principal and a group of three inspired parents. The school's mission was agricultural, with an emphasis on science and math. The approach had gone over very well with the rural community, and the school's enrollment had increased from 96 in its initial year to 340 in its fourth year. Over the course of four years, the school had gained a solid reputation for growth and achievement and was beginning to rival some of the best public schools in the county. With word getting out about his school's success, Trenton was starting to get job offers from other schools wanting his time and talent for their systems.

An offer from a science-focused urban school in Cleveland caught his attention. The model seemed to align with his mission and values, and after four years of serving as an assistant, he felt he was ready to run his own show. So, signing on as a new leader, he packed his bags and headed to the big city.

On arrival, Trenton was treated like royalty. The previous principal had left abruptly at the end of the contract year. Left in a lurch, the school needed a new leader, and Trenton appeared to everyone as the incoming hero. After the excitement of his arrival, however, Trenton soon found out the situation was worse than he had realized. While he knew the school had been on the decline, he didn't know it was facing closure if it couldn't find a way to reverse its downward academic trend. The community had embraced the school since its inception and was excited for the new leadership but becoming wary of the rumors of a shutdown. The school was also beginning to receive more systematic progress reviews, with formal notices of pending action in preparation for the potential reality of having to permanently close.

Given the hole he found himself in, Trenton carefully orchestrated preservice training during the summer, inspiring his team with enthusiasm, collaborative coaching, and hours of professional development from consultants specializing in the school's core content areas. Once the school year started, though, nothing seemed to work, and Trenton was quickly underwater.

By the third week of school, Trenton found himself in a whirlwind of desperate decision making. Systems and processes that he had developed in rural Ohio were tanking in Cleveland's urban core. His highly idealistic methodology for instruction and implementation was getting lost in a constant struggle with school culture and classroom behavior. As a result, suspension rates were sky high, and the phone never seemed to stop ringing. His office manager resigned after the second week, no longer willing to take the brunt of parent frustrations, and registration documentation was a mounting nightmare. His email inbox became unmanageable, and his inability to respond to school needs was painfully visible.

By January, Trenton was a shell of his former self. He had convinced himself, as a personal defense mechanism, to spend more time in his office, trying to create better response systems. Inevitably, though, he'd resign himself to calling back upset parents and doing his best to answer the never-ending string of staff questions. Every time he felt himself getting ahead, he'd be interrupted by a staff issue or student emergency. Each night, he'd return home and try to catch up with work left unfinished, but there were never enough hours in the day.

Trenton left his Cleveland school after one year. The school closed a year later. He now serves as the Midwest regional sales representative for a large textbook company.

> **Pause & Reflect**
>
> What concrete steps could Trenton have taken earlier in his tenure at his new school to avoid such a steady decline?

Maggie's and Trenton's stories aren't atypical. Their realities are repeating themselves all around us, especially in the inner city (Metzger, Fowler, & Swanstrom, 2018) where students need consistent, quality leaders and teachers the most. The first year for a new school leader is always challenging (Beam, Claxton, & Smith, 2016), and that challenge is made exponentially harder when arriving in an unfamiliar building with unfamiliar staff. Whether in a traditional public school, public charter school, or private school, navigating new leadership is daunting. In the field of group dynamics, with the push and pull from hundreds (or thousands) of students, parents, staff, and community members, every single day presents nuanced challenges that require decisive yet contextually subjective action. Some leaders rise above the difficulties to become great examples and great role models for others to follow, but without a good plan and a sound knowledge base, survival rates in the initial years are low. According to the news organization Education Week, data available from a handful of states suggest that only about half of beginning principals remain in the same job five years later, and that many leave principalship altogether when they go (Viadero, 2009). With the average tenure of a school leader less than five years, there is a growing need for quick success, but there is no step-by-step manual. There is no perfect system to replicate.

Preparation for Leadership

The research is clear: consistent, sustainable leadership yields higher student achievement gains and higher earning potential for graduates (Bartoletti & Connelly, 2013). In other words, we need to reduce turnover and keep our leaders around long enough to yield results. But data suggest that 18 percent of U.S. principals turn over each year (Bartanen, Grissom, & Rogers, 2019). School leaders need to be at their school at least five years for the full impact of their change efforts (systems, recruitment, retention, professional development, culture, and so on) to mature (Louis et al., 2010; McAdams, 1997). In response to these realities, this book offers systems and strategies for navigating the early years of a leadership change.

While it's a clichéd sentiment, great leaders are not born, but developed (Nauert, 2015). According to University of Illinois professors Kari Keating, David Rosch, and Lisa Burgoon (2014), "70% of leadership capacity is built through experience, not through genetic expression" (p. 3). As such, it's important to infuse strategy and focus into the school leader's developmental journey. New leaders will be tempted to reach for guidance from multiple sources, seeking singular answers for creating and leading the perfect school model. They might attend conferences and trainings, read books and articles, or listen to the insights and opinions of others in the profession. After all, anyone in a new role should do his or her due diligence in preparing for the new position. Since combining advice from a variety of sources can be overwhelming, contradictory, and confusing, we've developed this book as a comprehensive, practical tool kit. What we have learned and continue to experience in countless schools across the world serves as a guide for new leaders or veteran leaders in a new school or evolving setting.

The disparate approach of preparation programs, mentors and district leaders, sophisticated programs, and libraries of materials often bewilder new leaders; our approach to great leadership is one simple, well-focused path: a focus on strategic systems. Our combined experience teaching and leading in traditional public, charter, and private schools points to this focus on strategic systems. While it might be tempting to seek the silver bullet or the shiny, avant-garde school model, real success is founded on the development and effective deployment of strategic cultural, academic, and operational systems. Research tells us that students achieve higher scores on standardized tests in schools with leaders focused on strategic systems that create and support healthy learning environments (MacNeil, Prater, & Busch, 2009). The National Policy Board for Educational Administration (2015) explains:

> Educational leaders exert influence on student achievement by creating challenging but also caring and supportive conditions conducive to each student's learning. They relentlessly develop and support teachers, create positive working conditions, effectively allocate resources, construct appropriate organizational policies and systems, and engage in other deep and meaningful work outside of the classroom that has a powerful impact on what happens inside it. (p. 1)

With this concept of developing and deploying systems as the foundation, this book will offer strategies to approach your principalship in a way that directs you along a focused path. We'll push you to learn about the nuances of your school community and remain steadfast on your own strategic path to leadership success. We hope this book will help you avoid some of the more common missteps that happen during times of change for many K–12 principals. Whether you are brand new to the role of principal, an experienced leader in a new job or opening a new school, or a returning leader in a changing environment, you will find what you need here.

How to Use This Book

This resource will help new leaders go beyond merely surviving the constant deluge of needs in education. We provide an informative and strategic look at how new school leaders or veteran leaders in evolving settings can quickly develop tools to build on best practices; to leverage creativity without sacrificing growth; to manage and delegate tasks; to avoid reactive processes by replacing them with data-driven, proactive systems; and to understand the importance of a strong, calm, supportive school community.

Throughout this book's eight chapters, we provide you with personal accounts, firsthand lessons we have learned from our own career experiences, opportunities for reflection, and end-of-chapter reflection questions—all intended to help you strategically focus your initial years in your new school leadership position. You may want to dive right in and read this from cover to cover, or you may want to digest one salient point at a time. As you saw in The Challenges of Becoming a Principal (page 3), there are multiple opportunities in the book that invite you to pause and reflect without disrupting the flow of the reading. Whether used as a book study for cohorts of administrators or as a personal guide through leadership change, we encourage you to write your own ideas in the margins, share discussion points with colleagues, highlight what has personal meaning, and revisit each chapter as those challenges arise in your workplace.

Chapter 1 focuses on understanding the setting of the school that you're preparing to lead. It prepares you for understanding your building, your budget, key staff, stakeholders, and personnel. We recommend you read this chapter in the early summer to prepare for the coming year. Once the hectic, crazy rush of the first few weeks calms down, this is a good chapter to revisit as a checklist for evaluating the functionality of your system.

Chapter 2 is a must-read prior to opening in the fall, as it explores logistical concerns and preparing staff, students, and families for school to start. This section is best for late summer as you plan preservice training and implementation in the upcoming school year. This is also a good reference for the members of your leadership team as they prepare for the demands of opening day.

Chapter 3 takes a deep dive into relationships to help you navigate the subtle complexities that can trip you up in the opening months. This chapter will help ground your focus around the mission and vision, as well as the importance of community engagement. It is a great September reminder of how to cope with the pressures you're facing from a multitude of stakeholders.

Managing the entire site-level school operation is a nonstop and taxing process. Chapter 4 discusses proper task delegation and systems planning as keys to positive momentum. A quick skim through this chapter in the summer can help provide some context for the work that needs to be done throughout the year, but this is a great chapter to examine more closely over fall or winter break.

Chapter 5 explores the complexities of creating strong norms and behavior-management systems. This journey takes persistence and structure. Use this chapter to help unpack your understanding of implementation in the summer, but return to it after your systems are in place. Give this chapter a hard look over the winter break and determine whether there are changes you'd like to implement when you return in January.

Chapter 6 reviews considerations around curriculum, instruction, and assessment. Learning models and teachers' implementation styles can make massive differences in student outcomes, so one of a leader's most important responsibilities is ensuring consistent teacher quality. Consider coming back to this chapter over spring break as you think about addressing shifts that could have a larger impact in the years to come.

Chapter 7 focuses on staffing and management. There's only one of you, so you'll need to leverage your knowledge of best practices in a way that your staff can understand and implement. Later in the year, as you evaluate which of your staff members should be elevated into leadership and which may need urgent improvement, consider the lessons in this chapter around asset-based management. They are a great confidence booster in late April as you begin planning for next year's staffing needs.

Finally, the information in chapter 8 will heighten your ability to manage both the school budget and high-dollar federal grants, which will be critical to your success. This chapter covers the basics and offers suggestions for some simple bookkeeping practices that can keep you in a strong cash position. As federally reimbursable grants and school line items begin to spend down, this chapter acts as a late fall and early spring reminder of how to conceptualize and operationalize finances. It also serves as a helpful overview for the upcoming year's budget process.

To support your implementation of the concepts presented in each chapter, the appendix provides checklists, budgeting templates, and other resources you can use as you manage the many tasks of school leadership. Our desire is for the chapters and tools that follow to serve as your road map for strategically approaching your new position so that you can truly lead from the moment you take the helm. To begin this journey, we will focus on understanding the landscape of your specific school setting.

CHAPTER 1
Understand the Setting

You've been handed the keys to your school. Your principalship has moved beyond theory into practice. Remember to stay focused on determining your simple yet strategic plan, despite the temptation to settle in slowly. Introductions and relationships will be important, too, but one of your very first priorities is to quickly learn all you can about the type of school you're leading. In order to determine your core priorities, you first need to understand the landscape. In particular, what kind of school is it, and how should you find your bearings?

What Kind of School Are You Leading?

Different kinds of schools bring with them nuanced organizational structures and operational perceptions. For a new leader or veteran leader in a new setting, the first and most obvious question to ask is, "What kind of school is it?" Excluding preschools, boarding schools, home schools, colleges, and universities, there are some common school types in the United States. They are as follows.

1. **Traditional public schools:** These are publicly funded schools, divided into grades and governed by school districts, provincial governments, or townships. They are open to all students who live within the area they serve.

2. **Magnet public schools:** While still under district authority, a magnet school typically attracts students from across the normal boundaries or school zones inside a traditional public school district to a more specific or individualized school model.

3. **Charter schools:** These schools are still public schools receiving government funding, but they operate independently of the local traditional public school system.

4. **Private schools:** Sometimes called independent schools, these schools are typically free of state or federal regulation. They are privately funded and charge tuition for attendance.

For the purposes of this book, we're going to refer to magnet schools within the context of traditional public schools since they are generally incorporated into a traditional public school system. We describe each type of school in more detail in the following sections.

Public Schools

The category of traditional public schools refers to schools that students attend based on geography and the school district boundaries that are assigned to their home address. These schools typically receive local, state, and federal government funding, and students are not required to pay tuition. Faculty and staff who work in this category of schools also commonly have collective bargaining units and teachers' associations.

When it comes to public schools, the larger the school, the less flexibility you're likely to have as a leader. In a very small school or district, such as some in rural areas, the principal may have responsibility and flexibility similar to that of a charter or private school leader. In a large school or district, your staff may belong to a teachers' union with very standardized expectations for daily responsibilities. The district may have set your budget for you and limited your financial flexibility. Your school likely uses the same curriculum as a host of other schools in the district. Your managed services like food, janitorial, technology, and so on are likely handled at the district level. School schedules, busing times, daily class periods, and lunch schedules are likely set in stone.

Within large, traditional school districts, there may be magnet schools that provide an alternate option for parents within the district's geographical borders. Magnet schools typically specialize in a particular school model or approach to learning such as the performing arts or STEM (science, technology, engineering, and math), for example.

Charter Schools

The term *charter schools* typically refers to schools that have an authorizing agency that approves their model or written charter according to a specific list of required criteria and authorization processes unique to the state or province in which they reside. Charter schools typically have far more autonomy than their traditional public school counterparts. They can receive local, state, and federal funding but also rely on various fundraising efforts. Charter schools sometimes have teachers' associations or unions, but tend to be more independent of larger organizations.

Within charter schools, your staff are likely accustomed to the leader setting the tone of the day-to-day responsibilities. Your budget may have been set by the board in the prior year, but management of the budget requires your ongoing oversight and discretion. You probably approve expenditures with monthly board oversight, and you'll have input in the creation of next year's budget. Staffing decisions and salary negotiations are in your hands. Managed services and subcontractors may require your supervision and approval. The building and all surrounding property are probably yours to manage. Curriculum decisions are made at the school level with board approval, and calendaring, scheduling, busing, and so forth are likely all local decisions.

Private Schools

The category of private schools typically includes schools that parents choose to enroll their students in and that require tuition for attendance. Outside of voucher systems, private schools do not typically receive any funding from the local or federal government and they typically have far more autonomy than their traditional public and public charter school equivalents. Private schools do not typically have collective bargaining units or teachers' unions.

If you're in a private school setting, funding is the dominant mechanism driving your ability to effect change. As a school leader, you'll be heavily involved in the process of recruiting donors and funding the organization. You'll work closely with a director (either someone on the board or an administrator for the organization) to manage the fundraising, voucher, and enrollment processes. Parents will play a much bigger role in your school, as they represent a large portion of your donor base, and they often have high expectations for the success of their students. Your school will have a very strong, defined mission, and you'll work closely with your board to ensure budgeting allocations and daily operations align with that organizational mission.

Because private schools are not typically a teachers' union environment, budget projections will also drive your salary scale and competitive advantage in terms of staffing caliber. You likely have local control of scheduling busing, the hours of your instructional day, and staffing, but you will make operational decisions in tandem with a director or alongside board oversight. The board or parent committees often manage the facility and physical plant, but you will be expected to attend many, if not all, meetings.

In these descriptions of the three main school categories, you can see how understanding the type of school you work in will clarify the areas you can and can't control. Regardless of the type of school, it will be important to learn to focus on those areas you can control and winning those battles so the rest of the chaos doesn't overwhelm you.

What Kind of Leader Came Before You?

Whether you're taking on the principalship at a traditional public school, charter school, or private school, it's crucial to quickly learn the leadership history of the building. Determining whether you are following a successful or unsuccessful predecessor will determine your initial action steps as the new leader of a school. Your approach may differ depending on whether you are building on a tradition of high achievement that requires you to continue the best practices that are already in place or trying to correct a pattern of failure that requires deeper analysis and a strategic change in direction.

A helpful tool for this inquiry process is the Leadership for Learning Framework found in teaching and leadership consultant Douglas Reeves's 2006 book *The Learning Leader*. Reeves provides a matrix that compares student achievement results to factors that influence those results:

> As the matrix suggests . . . if there are high results that are accompanied by low understanding of the antecedents of excellence, the leader is not good but merely lucky. Such results are unlikely to be replicated. If the results are low and the antecedents of excellence are poorly understood, then we are doomed to a losing cycle of repeating the same actions and expecting different results. This quadrant of the matrix describes innumerable schools and entire systems where leaders will jump on every bandwagon and pursue every fad, but steadfastly refuse to make fundamental changes in scheduling, assessment, grading, personnel assignments, and leadership practices. They will change everything except, of course, those things that matter most for the results they want. (pp. 6–7)

For further understanding of Reeves's matrix and its application, see figure 1.1.

	Lucky	**Leading**
Achievement of Results	High results, low understanding of antecedents Replication of success unlikely	High results, high understanding of antecedents Replication of success likely
	Losing	**Learning**
	Low results, low understanding of antecedents Replication of failure likely	Low results, high understanding of antecedents Replication of success likely

Antecedents of Excellence

Source: Republished with permission of ASCD, from The Learning Leader *by Douglas Reeves, 2006, p. 6; permission conveyed through Copyright Clearance Center, Inc.*

Figure 1.1: The Leadership for Learning Framework.

The goal is to be a leader on the right side of the matrix in the Learning and Leading quadrants. A principal in the Learning quadrant says something like this:

> I've analyzed the data deeply, and here are my thoughts. First, although our average scores are disappointing, I've noticed that we have exceptional success in some isolated areas. Mr. Jasper's fourth graders excel in geometry, and Ms. Fitch's second graders made enormous gains in vocabulary. I've conducted some deeper observations of both their classes and found that they're engaging in some remarkably different teaching and classroom assessment practices. Our collective challenge is to conduct a treasure hunt and find other pockets of excellence, and then determine how we can identify, document, and replicate those practices.

The Learning principal is on the right path. Consider, however, that the Leading principal enjoys the benefit of high results along with a deep understanding of the antecedents of excellence. That principal has determined the adult actions (such as teaching, curriculum, and leadership practices) that have yielded successful student results, making replication of continued success likely (Reeves, 2006). As a principal in a new setting, you have to strive to be in the Leading quadrant. Whether your school has a history of high or low achievement results, it is essential to analyze the antecedents of those results in order to know where you should begin as the new leader. The following sections describe how you might respond to a successful or unsuccessful predecessor, as well as considerations for leaders in brand-new schools.

Following Success

Perhaps you find yourself the new principal of a school with a rich history of success. If so, the existing staff and district leadership will likely expect you to honor the traditions of pedagogy and culture that have led to the school's success. You may have grand aspirations that you can't wait to unveil, but until you pay homage to the individuals and antecedents of the school's successful past, no one will be interested in listening to your plans for the future.

In order to maintain respect, acknowledge past actions, and hopefully replicate previous success, you'll need to do some research and find the source of the success. According to Reeves (2006), replication of success comes through a pattern of high achievement results coupled with a deep understanding of the actions that yielded those results: "We must ask, 'Where are we good, and why did we get that way?'" (p. 135). Different teaching and leadership practices have varying impacts on student learning, so the key is to make "a systematic inquiry into the practices . . . that combine outstanding student results with systematic documentation of their teaching and leadership practices" (p. 135).

Make the investment in learning and honoring the existing leadership and teaching practices that have proven to be successful for the students in your school. Ideally, you've conducted some of this research prior to accepting the principalship and you support the school model, or at least the core components of it. It would be extremely difficult to push a new model on the staff when the existing one is working. This sounds obvious, but too often we press for change in our workplaces to prove we can add value. Trying to fix what already works is a dangerous mindset if left unchecked in successful environments.

In a school with a history of success, you should also be careful with references to your past work in other schools. Starting a proposal with, for instance, "At Elmcrest we used to . . ." is at best irrelevant and at worst disrespectful to the staff in your new school. Focus on the present and what you can do to help the staff continue their effective practices.

> **Pause & Reflect**
>
> How much change have you introduced or will you introduce into your new school setting? Given your school's past, present, and strategic future, are you trying to change too much or too little?

Cleaning Up Failure

Following a poor leader has its benefits. The good news is you can only go up from here! If you've received the keys to a school that has a history of failure, it's still critical to understand the antecedents of those results. What worked, and what didn't? Why? There's a ton to be learned from what didn't work in the past as you begin to determine what will work in the future. However, it's critical in building relationships with your staff that you always remain positive when referring to their past actions and their previous leader. Even though they didn't achieve a pattern of success, it's still important to respect the decisions that were made before you.

As you learn more about your new staff and their past, they will learn about your character and how you'll respond in a tough situation. They will learn a lot about your integrity and who you are as a leader by how you lead them through this adversity, together. Even though the school's data do not demonstrate a history of success, the staff almost certainly had good intentions. They were doing the best they knew how to do. Now it's your charge to build on that, honor their failed attempts, learn from those mistakes, and lead them toward a vision of strategic success.

Opening a Brand-New School

You've helped found or been hired as the first leader of a new school. You have a new staff with no prior conceptions or preconceived notions. All your decisions must be based on best guesses, predictions, extrapolation from other settings, and knowledge from experts and researchers. This situation has many potential pitfalls. Like a new teacher in a classroom of seasoned students, if you don't clearly define expectations and culture, you can easily lose control.

Regardless of the type of school, new settings require incredible strength and vision from the leader. In these settings, you'll want to hire your staff leadership far in advance and begin planning for the first year in every possible detail. In particular, you and your leadership team must predict and overcome as many foreseeable logistical roadblocks as possible, including bus schedules, food service timing, security services, classroom enrollment, and so on. Advance planning will prevent these issues from crashing the system during the first weeks of the school year, leaving you free to focus on academics, behavior, culture, parents, and so on. Initial relationships with this leadership team will be key. Preservice training for teachers whenever time and funding allow will provide an additional edge. Consider special summer sessions for staff to lock in the curricular models and implementation design to give your classrooms the head start they need.

What Are You Working With?

Once you get through the initial deluge of introductions, access codes, and human resources paperwork, you'll finally have your first chance to explore your facility. This experience can either resemble a dizzying walk through a hall of mirrors or be a tactical, eye-opening lesson on what needs to be improved. This is not a process to be taken lightly—a well-managed facility can have significant impacts on future student success (Hewitt, 2017). Consider the following story based on our experiences.

> In my first administrative position as an assistant principal, I was given the keys to the school in late May. It felt cool to have the keys to the kingdom, but without knowing any better, I drove home and waited to be called into professional development closer to the start of the school year. Boy, did I miss out on an opportunity to know my building! I started the academic year still trying to navigate to the right hall and find the right classroom. Many years later, I look back on that with regret.

Learn from this lesson. For a new leader, there is little time to waste. Learn your facility and review your budget to understand your new setting.

Learning the Facility

Your first priority is to get your bearings and identify some key elements of the physical plant. An initial walkthrough checklist found in the appendix (page 172) can help guide and focus this discovery process. Each day for a new leader is busier than the last, so having a guide to understand building functionality and facility potential is key to an efficient start. Hopefully, you are receiving the keys to your new school prior to the start of the school year. There is both a beauty and a weight that comes with that bundle of keys. Take a moment to bask in the greatness of your new home. Then invest substantial time exploring it. Grab a map and get lost in the building. Wander every hallway and peek behind every door.

Think about how the structure and layout of the building can maximize student achievement, and how your facility's functionality can make a strong positive or negative impact on learning. Poor lighting, odd noises, bad air quality, and inadequate heating in the classroom are significantly related to lowered student achievement (Cheryan, Ziegler, Plaut, & Meltzoff, 2014). In fact, over half of the schools in the United States operate within buildings that are inadequate; students of color and students from lower socioeconomic backgrounds are more likely to be found in buildings in need of help (Cheryan et al., 2014). This issue persists beyond the United States. In the United Kingdom, for example, comparisons between student performance and building issues such as indoor air quality, acoustics, temperature, and toxic exposure confirm significant problems related to inadequate school buildings (Bluyssen, 2017).

Remember that as soon as students and staff enter the building, you're responsible for their well-being. You have to understand your building in order to utilize it responsibly and get the most out of it. Will you know where to go when someone reports a fight in the upper E hallway? Will you know how to reset the HVAC system if it shuts down? Will you be able to tell if the air quality is subpar? You need to start getting ready as soon as you can, because after students and staff arrive, you'll need to be able to respond instantly. You may not have time to ask for directions or look at a map. So, prior to the start of the school year, make the time investment to thoroughly learn your building layout. Even if your exploratory work is limited to school safety (Trosper, 2017), this is a critical investment you won't regret.

Reviewing Your Budget

You may not have been involved in creating the budget for your first year in your job, but you'll want to acquire a basic understanding right away. The following story sets the tone for this topic.

> I saw my school's budget for the first time in January of my first year as principal. While it seems impossible to have operated for five months without knowing the budget, things were kept from me until they were all of a sudden dropped in my lap. I've never worked harder or faster to understand and utilize a complex document than that moment in January, and it ended up being some of the most important work of my career.

Beyond a quick snapshot, the annual budget will require a great deal of work and is something worthy of its own book. However, getting a general sense of the budget situation is a key aspect of understanding your setting. To better frame expectations behind the budgeting process, we've included a guide for basic budget considerations in the appendix (page 175). That guide provides some general benchmarks for the budget process.

Control over the budget will vary from site to site, but the least amount of control happens in more traditional settings. In larger, traditional public schools, leaders typically have very little control over a budget. It is very common for a district-level central office to determine budgets for each building and hold the purse strings. The principal's responsibility for budgeting in these schools is usually a simple matter of managing spending within a defined budget. While principals in these situations are free from the burden of controlling pots of money and maintaining lengthy spreadsheets, there is a feeling of powerlessness when it comes to funding resources and programming that you know your staff and students need. If you find yourself in this type of setting, prepare to become fluent in proposal writing as you'll need to defend your requests for building-level funds on an ongoing basis. It also helps to stay on good terms with the staff of the district finance department.

In smaller settings like charter schools and private schools, leaders may have a great deal of subjective control over the operational budget and will need to get up to speed right after accepting the position. While staffing will automatically use a majority of the budget, it's still important to understand the current salary schedule and look over individual salary amounts. After salary, review other programs that quickly erode budgets, such as curriculum, facilities, building improvements, technology, sports, food, and subcontractors. Then it's time to understand your cash position.

According to Avani Parikh and colleagues (2017), your unrestricted *days cash on hand* (DCOH) reflects your financial flexibility and capability to withstand financial problems while still covering operating expenditures. A stronger (higher) DCOH metric can mean greater resources at your disposal as you maintain the operation. To better understand the DCOH position of your school, you can conduct some simple calculations that may provide insight. Using a copy of your approved budget, follow these four steps to estimate your school's basic financial position.

1. Divide all total budgeted expenses by twelve months. This will give an approximate monthly cost for the organization.
2. Divide the total budgeted expense by 365. This will provide an approximate daily cost of operation.

3. Look at the estimated total annual expenses. Subtract that figure from the total estimated income. This will give you the remaining estimated cash for the end of the year.

4. Divide the estimated remaining cash (step 3) by the daily cost of operation (step 2) to see how many days cash on hand the organization plans to have at year's end.

Those four steps are certainly oversimplified. Other factors concerning debt, depreciation, or restricted funds can convolute the process of real cash on hand. For a new leader, however, this is a good first look.

In traditional public schools, the DCOH should balance very close to zero at the end of the year. Any negative balance will be seen as a critical error by district administration. Private and charter budgets factor differently. The initial years of a private or charter school can be lean, with a DCOH between ten and thirty days, which is certainly not a comfortable position. Any small school (one hundred to four hundred students) open for more than two years should have between thirty-five and seventy-five DCOH. For construction or enhancements, most lenders prefer to see at least ninety DCOH. After running through this four-step process at established schools, new leaders should be on alert if the cash position appears too low. If the DCOH results are below ten days, share the concern and enlist the help of the board, executive director, CEO, or other authorizer to improve financial planning process moving forward.

Whom Are You Working With?

Perhaps the most important aspect of getting to know your school is getting to know your team and your community. This includes learning about your staff, identifying external stakeholders and partners, and reviewing data to learn about your student population.

Leveraging Your Staff

It's important to remember that every professional in your school community is unique. The existing collective of experience and talent is not necessarily a mirror image to your own background and skill set. In order to get the most out of your system, you'll need to maximize the talents of those around you. Consider the following story as an example of what can happen if leaders fail to take this approach.

> When I started out as principal, I knew I had some great teachers on staff, but the more important task for me was to make sure my teachers understood how I wanted them to teach. My implementation style was unique, but I'd perfected it and it was highly effective for me. I had a great bag of tricks, and I mandated my model and style be replicated schoolwide. I couldn't wait to teach that forward, but in my zeal for innovation and my need to drive home pedagogy, I learned a valuable lesson. I could never clone myself. My teachers were lost in the process of trying to copy me. They already had an identity, and I had ignored it. It took me three years to recover from that mistake.

Whether walking into a well-established school or a first-year school with a completely new staff, it's critical to understand the pre-established systems, curriculum, and human capital already surrounding you. The proven systems and leaders in those environments should be leveraged to assist you in professional development, grade-level trainings, and implementation of the school model. Additionally, if there are staff members with obvious expertise outside of their current job description, consider whether a job change could benefit these people and the school. Lastly, while new leaders need to be strong, don't ignore the counsel of your staff.

In terms of teacher training, leaders too often hire multiple outside groups to come into a transitional environment and provide training. This is never more evident than the week before school starts each year. But think about this: with new leadership, you have a staff that is already suffering from transitional stress. Adding more unknown entities to the process may not provide the intended benefit. To create stability, do your best to limit the number of one-off trainings. If you want to bring in outside professionals, schedule ongoing trainings throughout the year. This lets your staff know that there will be a continuing relationship, and that these trainers will provide value. If you find that there are staff leaders capable of receiving training in advance and then delivering that training to the rest of staff, then consider that path. Peer delivery in a train-the-trainer model is more likely to create buy-in and can lead to higher academic potential (Ronfeldt, Farmer, McQueen, & Grissom, 2015).

Leadership is not a do-everything position—you do not need to change or influence everything right away. There has to be a balance of doing, delegating, observing, listening, and coaching. Leverage the talent already on site and take advantage of the tried-and-true practices already working in the system. This approach reduces the burden of reinventing the wheel and allows for a smoother path forward.

Understanding Stakeholders and Partners

No school operates in a vacuum, so be sure to ascertain the existing partnerships between your school and the local community. Failing to do so can lead to missed opportunities, as shown in the following story.

> **Missed Connection**
>
> It was late May, and Nick Douglas was the outgoing principal at a local elementary school. While his school had struggled academically, leading to his contract nonrenewal, he had developed strong community connections through a group of influential parents. In the previous year, those parents had connected him with a local hospital, set up a service-learning connection, and solidified an annual donation process. A new playground project was in the works, and a much-needed grounds renovation was moving to the design phase. In his angst over losing his job, however, Nick informed hospital administrators of his situation and suggested they discontinue their partnership to support efforts at his new school instead.
>
> Janet Lin, Nick's replacement, only found out about the hospital partnership in September, after being approached by a group of parents at the year's first parent-teacher organization meeting. By then four months had passed, and despite Janet's attempts at rekindling the relationship, the hospital had completed donation allocations and was unable to offer support. While hospital staff were polite to her, they had lost confidence in the relationship because of unstable leadership and lack of communication. After Janet returned news of the failed partnership to the parents, they quickly soured, blaming her for the loss of their renovation and playground projects.

Unless you're taking on a position in a brand-new school, there are inevitably leaders in the existing culture who, simply by their tenure and long-standing presence in the school community, have a type of legacy ownership in the establishment. In other words, these teachers, staff members, board members, community partners, or parents may wield a great deal of influence. These are the people you'll want to interview to understand your school and its place in the community. To find them, you'll want to ask some of the following questions when you arrive.

- "Who are the senior teachers and staff members?"
- "Who worked most closely with the previous leader?"
- "What outside organizations have relationships with the school?"

- "Are there any founding members still with the organization?"
- "Who are the annual donors or contributors to the school?"

The answers to these questions will yield a list of current stakeholders for your organization. Interviewing these stakeholders will provide perspective from those who hold a vested interest in your efforts. They may offer positive or negative feedback about the school and add insight to the expectations for your leadership position moving forward. They are likely to outline existing partnerships and relationships that come with preloaded expectations. Once you have a sense of these situations, you'll need to vet them against the mission, vision, and benefit to your leadership, and then either re-establish or carefully readjust them.

As soon as invested school partners hear there is a new principal, they will want to make an appointment to meet with you—everyone wants time with the new principal. It sends a great message to your school community when you take the time to hold these types of meetings. More than anything, external partners want to feel heard and want to be given the opportunity to start or continue a relationship. Investing this time up front will allow you to begin determining good partnerships and recognizing questionable ones early on. Remember, just because a partnership existed in the past doesn't necessarily mean it will align with your vision for the future.

Beyond the key partners in your school community, there are likely building principals and leaders in your district or region willing to meet and share additional information. Your job is to leave no stone unturned. You must quickly assess the resources you have at your disposal against the resources you need. In other words, you're looking to identify and capitalize on partnerships that can benefit your cause. You also need to be able to turn down or weed out partnerships that inhibit your ability to grow. We'll further discuss how to assess the value of relationships in chapter 3 (page 49).

Reviewing Student Data

As you begin to understand your new setting, the data from your school will be a critical window into its academic and cultural inner workings. As they say, the numbers don't lie. Outside of brand-new schools, no site lacks data sources. In fact, there may be so much information that trying to merge the various reports into an insightful snapshot will likely pose the greatest challenge. We recommend that you focus your initial investigation on two categories: *academic data* and *demographic data*. In particular, consider the following data sets.

- Academic data
    - Proficiency in mathematics and English language arts (disaggregated by demographic subgroups)
    - Standardized test scores (ACT, SAT, state and province exams, and so on)
    - Discipline data (numbers of detentions, suspensions, and expulsions, disaggregated by demographic subgroups)
    - Attendance rates
    - Graduation rates
    - Special education (students with individualized education plans [IEPs] and 504 plans)
- Demographic data
    - Socioeconomic status (often represented by the number of students receiving free or reduced lunch)
    - Ethnicity
    - English learners
    - Gender

You'll want to disaggregate these data by grade level and compare your school to others in the district or network, and to similar schools in other parts of the state or province.

Your school's core academic and demographic data will answer many questions and help pave your journey for future action. There are several guiding questions you should seek to answer.

- At a glance, how is the school performing academically?
- Are there any grade levels or subgroups of students that are exemplars or outliers in their level of performance?
- Which grade levels or subgroups are lagging behind the others?
- Are all student demographic groups performing at a comparable level?
- What do the school's discipline data tell you? Are student demographic groups equally represented? Are the data similar by grade level?

After you have drawn your own conclusions regarding your school's academic and demographic data, it's important to understand how your district, network, or school board measures success. What are its criteria for a successful school? What are its conclusions on the school's current data? How does the school's current improvement plan align with the data?

As you dig deeper, learn all you can about the student population you've been called to serve. One of the most critical steps for a new leader is to truly know whom you serve. In order to plan the best program of study for your students, you must know who they are and what they need to be successful. What community of families do you serve? What are your students' needs? What are their backgrounds, and how do their backgrounds impact their learning? Too often, new leaders are tripped up by tailoring core instruction and interventions to the majority demographic group of their student population. However, it is the moral imperative of every principal to ensure high levels of learning for each and every student.

> **Pause & Reflect**
>
> Do you have a solid feel for the facility condition and stakeholder capability in your setting? What priority needs have you uncovered?
>
> How can you balance the infusion of your strategic leadership while still leveraging the ability and efforts of those around you?

Summary

Surveying your new environment is an essential first step toward success in your new principalship. As early as possible—ideally early in the summer before your first year as leader begins—start building your understanding of your school and its community. In this chapter, we discussed four important aspects you need to know about: (1) the type of school you're leading; (2) the school's leadership history; (3) the facility, budget, and data you've inherited; and (4) the people who will surround you. Making the effort to learn and understand will set a foundation for effective and informed leadership. In the next chapter, we describe a proactive approach to getting your facility, staff, and students ready for the first day of school.

Chapter 1 Reflection Questions

1. What is the landscape of your new school? What kind of school have you inherited in terms of structure, facility, finances, and demographics?

2. What kind of leader came before you? How will this impact you as the new leader?

3. Considering the past history and current setup of the school, what successful practices or relationships can you build on?

4. When considering facility, budget, and stakeholders, what are the most important factors for your initial planning?

5. What facts can you glean from the school's data to guide your planning efforts?

CHAPTER 2

Prepare for Opening Day

Moving forward to think about the opening days of the school year, the emphasis is on preparation. Preparation is simple, but it offers many challenges for school leaders. One of the busiest times of the year for a principal is (or should be) the summer. The preparations required to open for a new school year are extensive and include tasks related to logistics, staff, and students and their families. When preparing for opening day, the goal is to be meticulously prepared so you can quickly overcome the easy problems. That way, when the difficult problems appear (and they will), you have the time and capacity to handle them. With focus, teamwork, and effective time management, the beginning of the first year in a new building can be a great opportunity to spread your wings as a leader and show your staff and families who you really are.

Depending on the size and varying strengths of your leadership team, it is important to delegate tasks to the team members who have the most experience or expertise in each area. As the principal, you don't need to do all the work yourself—you just need to ensure that it gets completed. Maximize the strengths of the leadership team and front office staff in order to efficiently prepare for the opening of school. If you're inheriting a school with experienced leadership, listen to your team with regard to the procedures that have worked well in the past. For example, if you have evidence that many families typically attend the school's registration and schedule pickup day the week before school starts, allowing counselors to meet with new enrollees and distribute schedules in advance, by all means continue that practice. Make careful observations during the registration events to note what you may want to change for next year. This same principle can be applied to every back-to-school task. Learn from the experience and history of your team before you determine how to complete or delegate each task.

If you're opening a new school with new leadership, you'll be establishing procedures for the first time collectively. The best way to attack your list of preparations is to determine the most effective methods possible based on your knowledge and experiences in other schools. Keep in mind, however, that you may still have to make major changes next summer based on how smoothly (or not) school opens this year.

> **Pause & Reflect**
>
> How well do you know the strengths and weaknesses of your leadership team? What steps can you take to be sure they add value and lessen the burden of a successful school opening process?

Summer preparation work for the first day of school typically falls into four categories:

1. Preparing staff
2. Preparing the logistics
3. Preparing families
4. Preparing for special populations

The following sections detail these categories of action; a reproducible checklist appears in the appendix (page 177). Consider these tasks as you determine your leadership team's back-to-school checklist of responsibilities.

Preparing Staff

The days or weeks you are given to prepare your new staff for how you want your building to run is a critical time. How you prepare your staff for opening day will speak volumes to your team and set the initial tone for your leadership style. As you review the following list for preparing your staff for opening day, think about how many of these tasks you should own as the new principal and how many you should delegate to others on your leadership team or front office team. Your ownership or delegation of this preparation process will also send a strong message about your leadership style. Do you prefer to approach these preparations as a team, or do you prefer to lead with a "new sheriff in town" style? We can't overstate how important your initial communications with your staff are in terms of setting a tone for the new year and establishing your leadership identity with them.

- **Letter to faculty and staff:** We strongly recommend that you write a letter to your staff as their new principal. This is the perfect opportunity to set the tone as their leader. Consider including a "welcome back" message, a reiteration and strong endorsement of the school's mission, any important dates and meetings for the summer and the first month of the school year, and introductions of any new staff hired over the summer. Midsummer is an appropriate time to send this letter to staff members. This allows them ample notice for upcoming dates and meetings but also allows a few weeks of free time at the beginning of the summer before they have to start thinking about the next school year.

- **Any remaining hiring:** Complete the hiring of any new staff as quickly as possible. The longer you wait, the fewer quality applicants you will have. There are three main hiring windows during the education year, as shown in table 2.1.

Table 2.1: Three Main Hiring Windows

Hiring Window	Reasons for Availability	Typical Ability
January–March	These educators are usually midyear graduates and midyear relocations.	Midyear graduates are usually young but talented. Occasionally, you may find strong veterans relocating midyear.
April–June	These educators are typically making proactive decisions to look for a career move as they finish their year.	This is the prime hiring season for talented staff. This is also the season of hiring fairs and college graduate placement.
July–August	These educators did not find a placement in the prime hiring window or potentially had a recent life change. There is also the possibility they were recently let go from their former employer.	It can be more challenging to find quality candidates during this later window. Still, family relocation candidates or those who have self-selected out of a tumultuous setting can be great finds.

- **Faculty handbook:** A faculty handbook should contain all essential procedures and expectations for staff. If one exists, determine what updates you need to make. If your school does not currently have a handbook, you'll need to create one. This task can be very time consuming if you are starting from scratch, so begin this process early in the summer.

- **Opening faculty meeting:** This will be the first in-person impression you make on your new staff, so be very thoughtful regarding the messages and content you convey in your first all-staff meeting. Plan in advance what critical information you need to share with them prior to opening school, and stay focused by considering what can be tabled for future faculty meetings. Use this time to begin establishing your leadership style and rapport with your team. The opening faculty meeting should take place on the first teacher-report day for the new school year. This varies greatly depending on the school type. In some districts, teachers may report just days before students arrive, while in other schools, teachers report weeks prior to the first student day.

- **Professional development and teacher report days:** Find out how many days you get with your staff prior to the opening of school. When are they? How much time is at your discretion, and how many activities are required by your district or network? Prioritize use of the time at your discretion to equip your teachers with the tools they need to most effectively begin the school year.

- **Schoolwide and classroom-level procedures:** It is critical to explicitly teach students your expectations, both in the classroom and around the building as a whole. We will take a deep dive into developing procedures and expectations for this in chapter 5 (page 85), but it is important to note here that this preparation should be a significant part of your summer. You will need to develop the systems and plan training with your leadership team, and then train your staff prior to the first day of school. Any presentations to teach students the expectations must occur in the first few days of the school year.

Preparing the Logistics

Tackling this list of logistical tasks that must be completed prior to opening day will require a team effort. Some of the items on this task list can be delegated to support staff members such as secretaries or custodians, but many of them require administrative oversight or completion. We encourage you to be thoughtful about who is the best staff member to complete each task and to consider the length of time required to finish it before school starts. School will not open effectively without all of these logistical components in place.

- **Master schedule:** Depending on the size and complexity of your school, completing the master class schedule and balancing classes can be an all-consuming job or might simply require minimal maintenance over the summer. If you have an assistant principal who is the primary scheduler, check in with him or her frequently to ensure you agree with teaching assignments and class sizes for each course and grade level. Be sure to allow space in classes for students who move to your school late in the summer.

- **Master calendar:** Create a master calendar for the school year that shows all important events such as back-to-school night, parent-teacher conferences, report cards, vacations, and so on. Distribute this calendar to staff and families and make it readily accessible on the school website.

- **Classroom setup:** Inventory all classroom furniture, technology, nameplates, textbooks, supplies, and other materials, and order any needed replacements. It's critical to perform this task early in the summer to beat distributors' back-to-school barrage of orders.

- **Bus schedule:** If your school provides transportation for students, be sure you know the bus numbers, parking assignments, rosters of students on each bus, drop-off and pickup times, traffic flow, and the district's protocol for radio communication with drivers and the transportation department. Assign faculty to bus duty assignments based on the district's transportation safety protocol or make new guidelines for bus duty. Create or update a parking diagram that shows bus parking.

- **Traffic flow:** Determine a safe and orderly traffic route for drivers dropping off and picking up students.

- **Bell schedule:** If your school operates on a bell schedule using a traditional timed bell or public address (PA) system, confirm that the schedule is current, programmed, and functioning correctly. If there is no bell or PA system, determine the solution for consistent class movement throughout the day.

- **Locker combination rollover:** If your school has lockers with built-in locks, the combinations likely need to be changed before school begins. Typically, a custodian or administrator needs several days to complete this task.

- **Summer deep cleaning:** Coordinate with your head custodian or maintenance lead to ensure all required deep cleaning of the school is completed over the summer. For example, if classrooms have carpet and need to be shampooed one at a time, schedule a rotation so that all floors are cleaned and dry before teachers return to set up their rooms.
- **Interdepartmental communication:** Your food service, transportation, and maintenance staffs are some of the most critical people to befriend immediately. Ongoing two-way communication with these departments is essential. Their daily operations impact all of your students and staff, so communicate with them early and often to avoid confusion and headaches later.

Preparing Families

Similar to preparing staff for the opening day of school and setting the tone of your leadership style, your initial communications with families will establish your leadership identity. While it's important to acknowledge that some families may have particular needs that vary from others, in general, all families are likely to desire a caring, organized principal who is a great communicator. Prior to opening day, parents want to receive communication from you that welcomes them and makes them feel good about placing their child in your care. Students want to receive communication from you that makes them feel that you care about them and that you want to give them all the information they need in order to effectively navigate their first days of the school year. As you review the following list for preparing families for opening day, think about ways in which these tasks (and others you may want to add) convey that you and the staff care about your students and are well prepared for a successful school year.

- **Back-to-school packets and summer mailings:** It's helpful to deliver all important back-to-school information and forms to families by midsummer so they have time to prepare appropriately for the school year. If you are inheriting an existing school, consider adapting any documents that have been used successfully in the past to make things easier. Typical summer mailings include a "welcome back" letter from the principal, registration forms, emergency medical forms, a master calendar, and details regarding registration, schedule pickup, or meet-the-teacher events.

- **Registration and meet-the-teacher events:** Immediately before the opening of the school year—typically within a day or two of the first day of school—host a registration or schedule pickup event for students to locate the classrooms they will report to on the first day. In elementary schools, it's common to host an event like an ice cream social where students can meet their teachers and find their classrooms, desks, and cubbies. In secondary schools, it is more typical to host a registration or schedule pickup day for students to get their schedules and walk the building to find their classrooms and lockers. A meet-the-teacher night should take place a couple of weeks after school has started so that parents and guardians may meet their children's teachers.
- **Automated calls and emails to families:** Remind families of the registration and meet-the-teacher events as well as the first day of school via your automated phone message system, mailings, and emails. You cannot overcommunicate this information in the days leading up to the first school day.

Preparing for Special Populations

Because of its nuanced and specialized nature, school leaders may find themselves feeling anxious about leading the programming of special education services. With special education, there are many unique factors to oversee in order to have a successful program. And while it may seem impossible to be prepared for every angle of school leadership, special education deserves your prioritized attention. Preparing effectively to serve special populations of students is not only a moral imperative, but the legal aspects of this department require proper focus and diligence.

Familiarize Yourself With the Law

School leaders should have working knowledge of applicable laws governing the education of special populations. In our experience, the education law classes taught in graduate programs and administrative certifications do not provide sufficient training to navigate the legal context of special populations. This lack of training can create a knowledge deficit in incoming school leaders in the field of special education. While these graduate programs clearly recognize they have a responsibility to teach educators and administrators about the law, professors "rarely evaluate whether their students have comprehended the content" (Decker, 2014, p. 679). Janet Decker (2014) dubs this problem *legal illiteracy*; she outlines the issue by explaining that "legal illiteracy may result in unnecessary costs, while legal literacy can yield incredible benefits, including increased empowerment, improved ethical decision-making, and a better ability to fulfill job responsibilities" (p. 682). If principals are uninformed, they also risk spreading misinformation to staff. Whether students are in general education, English learners, or impacted by the Individuals With Disabilities Education Act, there is no denying the importance of properly supporting the rights and needs of all segments of your school population.

One simple way to learn more about special education law is to purchase and read relevant legal guidebooks. There are hundreds of publications highlighting the best practices for special populations in schools. For new leaders, we recommend two must-have publications.

1. *Wrightslaw: Special Education Law* (Wright & Wright, 2016)
2. Your state or province's special education law

If you need to locate your local special education law, visit your state or province's department of education website. Keep both of these resources close at hand for reference and general reading. You should also obtain the contact information for your special education counsel.

Familiarity with the law is an important aspect of protecting your school. The vast majority of school leaders want the best for every one of their students, but good intentions do not prevent lawsuits. Failure to meet the needs of special populations is a key element in many school lawsuits, which can cost schools tens of thousands of dollars per case. Verdicts against the school cost even more in fines and damages and could put the leader's job in jeopardy. In addition to knowing the requirements, leaders should plan proactively for universal access and an environment of equity.

Plan Proactively

Most school programs (academic and nonacademic) are geared to serving the general population and then reverse engineered sometime later to provide access to those with special needs. This backward approach typically creates a legal solution, but it's not always the most ethical or effective path. As a new leader, you'll have the opportunity to correct this trend. For instance, when choosing new curricula or determining extracurricular options, factoring in equitable access for all students from the beginning will lead to thoughtful integration and save potential headaches down the road. When it comes to buildings and physical facilities, state or provincial rules and city codes for construction dictate the importance of equal access for those with disabilities. School program development should be no different.

On arrival at your new position, you'll want to dig into your school's equity statement and special education plan. Most, if not all, schools will have a plan on file with the state or province. If you're leading a brand-new school, you may be quickly tasked with creating this plan. A school's equity plan should explain how the school promotes equitable access through a wide variety of approaches and allows access to all school programming regardless of any differentiating or handicapping condition.

Next, look to see if Universal Design for Learning (UDL) practices or policies are in place. For schools, UDL is a guide for the greater educational process, providing an equitable pathway for success for all students. UDL processes help to keep schools (from school design to educational implementation) flexible in their approach to facilities, systems, materials, supplies, and instruction. Review these school plans and policies so you have a solid understanding of what they intend to accomplish. If you're in a brand-new setting, work with your leadership team and special education staff to define UDL practices for your school.

Then, consider creating a mission statement for special education in your school. The National Center for Special Education in Charter Schools (2018), a national nonprofit focused exclusively in this field, outlines seven key principles for equitable schools: (1) accessibility, (2) inclusion, (3) quality, (4) collaboration, (5) accountability, (6) autonomy and flexibility, and (7) resources. These values form a useful framework for writing your mission statement; visit www.ncsecs.org/principles-of-equitable-schools to learn more about each one. The statement in figure 2.1 exemplifies how a school can prioritize equity.

To be successful in terms of access and equity for all student populations, we at Sycamore School believe there must be a combination of differentiated teaching and intentional resource support present that aligns closely with general education classroom instruction, providing students with the supports and accommodations they need. Our general educators will consider all students a part of their class rather than expecting special educators and counselors to be solely responsible for meeting specific needs of students with IEPs or ongoing individualized care. While all students may receive part of their instruction in the general education classroom, students can still receive part of their instruction as needed in a resource room. However, special education is a resource and not a place. Resourced instruction will always be working toward the same goals and concepts as the general education classroom.

All general educators at Sycamore School need to understand and affirm the basic IEP goals, 504 plans, English learner plans, modifications, and accommodations for the students in their classes. Furthermore, our paraprofessionals will be included in instructional planning by being physically present during meetings and having access to related online documentation.

Figure 2.1: Sample equity statement. continued ⇨

> The special education, counseling, multitiered system of supports (MTSS), and response to intervention (RTI) teams will assist administration by extending basic expectations and incorporating schoolwide communications around specialized learning plans. This team will give all teachers a short summary of their students' accommodations, goals, and needs, providing diverse pathways for support within the classroom. This means that while English learners and students with IEPs and 504s may have multiple teachers influencing their educational pathways, all teachers at Sycamore School are working toward the same measurable goals. Student learning can then increase through like-minded focus and intensity rather than becoming disjointed from shifting between a duality of general education and specialized education instruction.

This statement is broad, but plans like this help sharpen high-level policy into site-level guidance. With a few slight tweaks to the plan we've crafted here, new leaders can have a mission statement that provides a backbone for all overarching school programs.

As another example of planning and preparation, look at the flowchart in figure 2.2, which was developed for special education at a public charter school in Indianapolis, Indiana. This program document provides a sound overview of what a full year looks like for special education. Coming into your initial year at your new school, you will find a process like this one is a good starting point for a special education program. Having your special education leader craft a similar flowchart will help your program develop its own functional identity.

We cannot overstate the need for elevating the priority of access and equity in your systems and programs. As a new leader, a leader in a new school, or a returning leader in a new environment, you must proactively program for students who need additional supports. If the equity practices in your school aren't well thought out and well structured, there will be tension between you and special education students and their families. If you have a strategic system of supports for students with special needs, you'll garner stakeholder support and willingness to collaborate. There is no secret to serving special populations or solving parental concerns: intentionality and preparation are the path to success.

Summary

This chapter delineated key areas of preparation for the first day of school. Hire qualified candidates for any remaining positions and begin forming relationships with and providing professional development for your teachers and staff. Get logistical concerns like schedules and bus routes out of the way early so you can focus on

Prepare for Opening Day   41

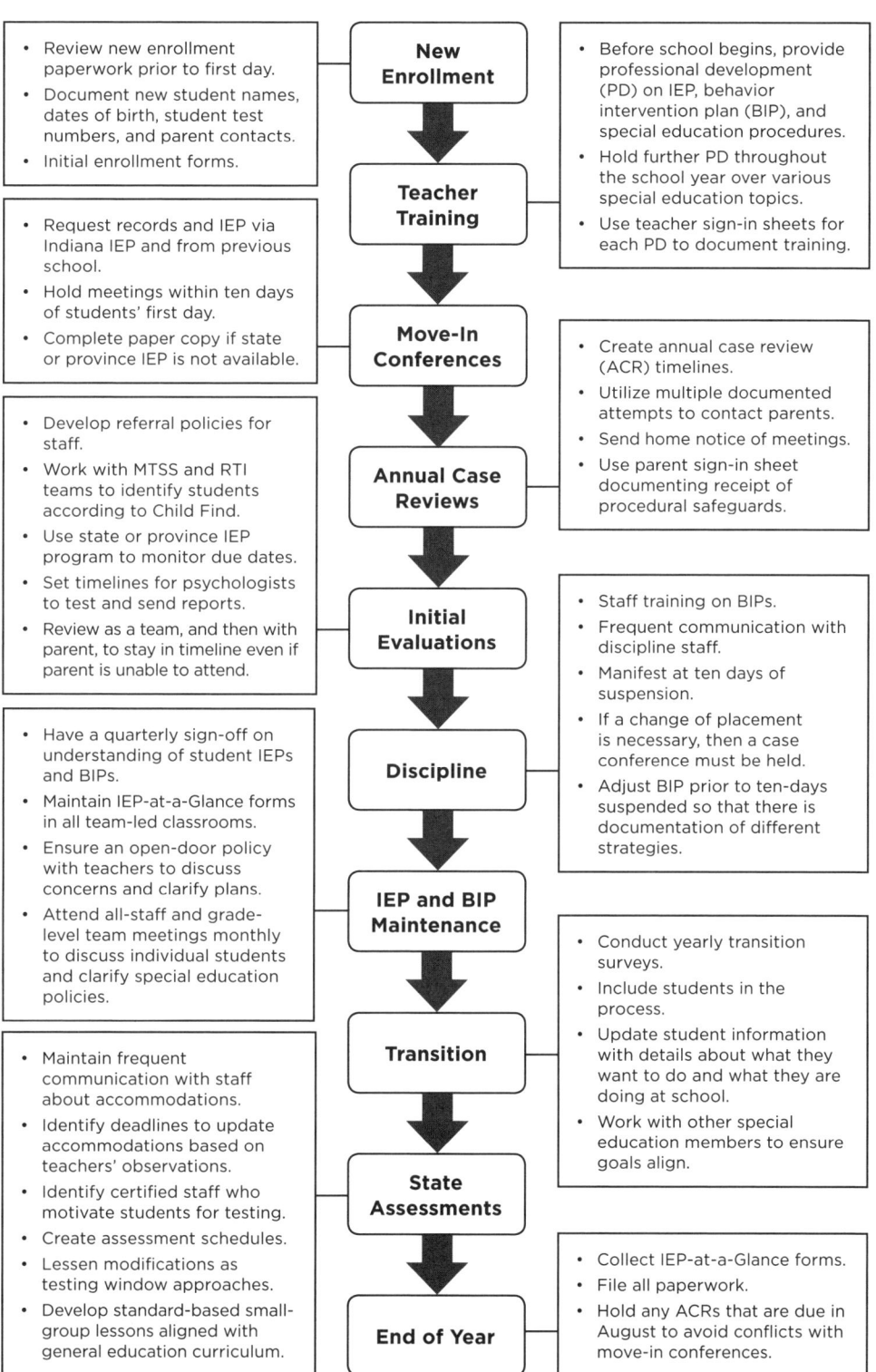

Source: © 2019 by Paramount Schools of Excellence. Created by Tommy Reddicks and Stefanie Hanes. Used with permission.

Figure 2.2: Sample special education flowchart.

supporting students. It's also important to reach out to your student community and give families adequate time to prepare for the upcoming year. Finally, plan to serve special populations of students by familiarizing yourself with the law and proactively establishing equitable systems. With these preparations in place, you'll be ready for a successful start to the school year. In the next chapter, we explore the importance of building educational relationships.

Chapter 2 Reflection Questions

1. What first impressions do you hope to make on your staff, parents, and students?

2. Review the checklist for preparing your staff for opening day (page 177). Which tasks will you complete? Which can you delegate to team members based on the strengths of your team?

3. Review the checklist for the logistical tasks that need to be completed before opening day (page 177). Which tasks appear to be the highest priority? Why?

4. Review the checklist for preparing families for opening day (page 177). Which tasks will you complete? Which can you delegate to team members based on the strengths of your team?

5. What special populations of students does your school serve? How prepared are you and your staff to meet their unique needs on the first day of school? What policies and resources do you need to put in place?

CHAPTER 3

Build Educational Relationships

We have been describing a variety of logistical tasks and considerations for the facility, but we'll shift now to the human side of education. While classroom teaching is an obviously personal and interactive endeavor, school leaders sometimes get distracted from educational relationships, as you can see in the following story.

> In the second week of my administrative licensure course, our cohort was reviewing articles on educational leadership. We had all just turned in our second paper on leadership, and I had waxed poetic, wasting the mandatory assignment space on great examples of leaders and the importance of educational design. The class conversation was all surface talk with cohort members showing off by proving what they knew, and the instructor continually walking the conversation back to his own practical experience. But, as the group's egotism spiraled, a colleague of mine leaned over, completely excited, and said, "All of this just keeps boiling down to relationships." I nodded my head, tuned out the discussion, and let his idea roll around in my brain for a while. The more I thought about it, the more I realized this wasn't just a one-off realization. Not only was he exactly right, but years later, no matter how simple the thought, it continues to ring true. This education thing is all about relationships!

There is an art and science to education. In this chapter, we focus on the art of relationships. In any setting requiring collaboration, which likely includes every business or industry in the world, success is dependent on relationships. Hard work matters, but without relationships, there is no outlet, proof, or approval for the work. The concept of *relationship* is complex. It has many layers and many definitions in the field of education. In this chapter, we break relationships into four leadership-related sections.

1. Emotional intelligence
2. Relationship evaluation
3. Fundraising and friend-raising
4. Community engagement

Principals are often subject to a barrage of people, organizations, and vendors, all vying for your attention and support. Area curriculum representatives will be making pleas for buy-in. Software companies will be begging to give demonstrations. Local businesses and organizations will be asking for advertisements or referrals. Even your teachers will be bringing their connections your way. Amid all these opportunities, you need to select, build, and maintain the ones that support your work and your school's growth. By the same token, you need to avoid the ones that may damage your school's integrity or degrade your position in the school. Managing relationships is one of the core practices of principals that separates the excellent leaders from the mediocre ones. The guidance in the following sections on the four aspects of relationships will help you navigate the challenge of connecting with people and amplify your know-how in leveraging relationships to benefit your school.

Emotional Intelligence

From top to bottom, education is built on and driven by people. Other professions might center on products or services, but our profession is defined by human outcomes; hence, education is a people business. The people in schools make or break the success of the organization. The students, staff, parents, and leaders who make up a school also define what *success* means to them in the particular context of their setting. No matter the angle from which we look into the organization, people and relationships are at the core.

Navigating the art of relationships begins the moment you arrive on the job. As the new principal, your staff will be sizing you up to determine your character, personality, and leadership style. Every interaction with a staff member individually or in a group provides an opportunity for you to project positive traits. Through both your verbal and nonverbal communication, you send countless messages on a daily basis. The higher the *emotional intelligence* of those receiving your communication, the faster they will form judgments (Jacob, Kreifelts, Nizielski, Schütz, & Wildgruber, 2016). Simply stated, emotional intelligence is "the capacity to be aware of, control, and express one's emotions, and to handle interpersonal relationships judiciously and empathetically" ("Emotional Intelligence," 2019). Establishing these viable working relationships with your staff early in your tenure is critical to the health and success of your team. In fact, *trusting relationships* was identified as a key factor for leadership effectiveness in "odds-beating schools" (Zuckerman, Wilcox, Durand, Lawson, & Schiller, 2017).

One of the most instinctual nonverbal messages you will send to your staff is whether you truly care. Do you genuinely care about the role you play and the responsibility you carry as the school leader? Do you care about your staff as professionals and as people? Do you care about their success? Just as teachers must demonstrate caring to their students in a firm yet supportive manner, principals must demonstrate the same to their staff. To some extent, your staff becomes a family. In your time together, you'll experience highs and lows—both professional and personal—as a group. Through it all, your staff will turn to you to guide them through these ups and downs while remaining steadfast as to the school's mission. All of these trials, tribulations, and celebrations provide the perfect opportunity to show them who you are as a leader and a person. Your staff will become a team and be willing to meet and exceed all your expectations because you've earned their respect and confidence in your leadership ability as a principal and a human.

To be clear, *caring* does not mean softening your standards of excellence, or asking staff to hold hands and share their feelings at faculty meetings, or any of the other caricatures one hears around the topic of emotional intelligence. We are talking about how leaders handle themselves and their relationships. As psychologist Daniel Goleman (2004) outlines in his article, "What Makes a Leader":

> It's not that IQ and technical skills are irrelevant. They do matter, but mainly as "threshold capabilities"; that is, they are the entry-level requirements for executive positions. But my research, along with other recent studies, strongly suggests that emotional intelligence is the sine qua non of leadership. Without it, a person can have the best training in the world, an incisive, analytical mind, and an endless supply of smart ideas, but he still won't make a great leader.

We can probably all think of leaders we've known who bring out the best in us and drive us toward a shared vision. Conversely, we can all point to leaders who are highly intelligent yet fail to move their teams to high levels of performance. The importance of relationships in effective leadership cannot be overstated; as Goleman's (2004) research poignantly explains, "the most effective leaders are alike in one crucial way: they all have a high degree of what has come to be known as emotional intelligence."

> **Pause & Reflect**
> What does a school leader with high levels of emotional intelligence look like? How can you apply this vision to your leadership setting?

Just how important is strong emotional intelligence to a leader? In Goleman's (2004) extensive review of competency models from 188 companies, he analyzed which personal capabilities drove outstanding performance by comparing purely technical skills to cognitive abilities and emotional intelligence. His findings concluded that, among factors contributing to excellent performance, "emotional intelligence proved to be twice as important as the others for jobs at all levels," and in fact, when Goleman compared the profiles of star performers with average ones, "nearly 90% of the difference in their profiles was attributable to emotional intelligence factors rather than cognitive abilities." In other words, the emotional intelligence of a leader outweighs all other skills and traits, hands down.

One of the most common ways that leaders exhibit their emotional intelligence is in how they manage themselves and their relationships with others. We call this *relationship agility* or, in other words, being able to maneuver your interactions and relationships with others in a manner that is agile and responsive. Excellent leaders are masters of finessing their interactions and responses to others based on an understanding of those individuals' needs. This is the human side of education—what makes it a people business. Although you need to remain steadfast in your strategic plans, what separates the excellent leaders from the mediocre ones is a balance between strategy and emotional intelligence.

In the same way that a teacher can be an academic who knows her content inside and out but can't relate to her students or build rapport with them, a disconnect can occur in leadership. All the strategies and intellect in the world are no substitute for relationship agility. Leaders have to keep the momentum moving forward, and a combination of trust and relationships increases your leadership capacity (L. Gardner, 2016). Principals must also find a delicate balance between the *what* and the *how* of leadership. While it's critically important to develop frameworks, standard operating procedures, and other systems, those systems require a leader who knows how to do the following.

- Push people toward enthusiasm and high performance
- Step on the gas while knowing when to pump the brakes

- Remain emotionally composed when a crisis strikes
- Create a healthy urgency to push toward higher achievement

These actions represent the emotional intelligence of a leader. In other words, when a principal appropriately balances effective actions with a caring, conscientious demeanor, he or she has the best chance of becoming a great leader.

Emotional intelligence permeates every aspect of your job, and every choice contributes to your relationship with your staff. As one example, consider how leaders spend their time. In *Leverage Leadership 2.0*, author and educator Paul Bambrick-Santoyo (2018) expounds on the finding that leaders in his study only spent 6 percent of their time involved with day-to-day instruction. This implies that up to 94 percent of a leader's time is spent on administrative tasks, something that often causes new leaders to lose control of their emotional connection to day-to-day staff. Even if they get everything else just right, leaders who fail in this primary task of attending to instruction and teachers will simply not have enough cohesion for things to work as well as they could or should. As you begin interacting with your new staff, think about the time you've allotted for connecting with them and attending to issues that matter to them. How are you mobilizing and motivating your team to action?

Relationship Evaluation

Every relationship is different, and each relationship comes with expectations. Some relationships are simple, like existing connections in the school, friends in the community, ties to area organizations, and so on. Others are more challenging, like incentive-driven resource access from major corporations, branding and logo partnerships, transportation contracts, construction bids, and the like. You need criteria to differentiate positive relationships from negative, whether complex or simple. This is where our concept of *measuring sticks*, or criteria against which you can evaluate relationships, comes in.

The first measuring stick to keep in mind when evaluating a relationship is its impact on the mission and vision of your organization. For instance, if your school has a focus on project-based education and you're approached by an engineering firm to partner and collaborate on design projects, you may have found a relationship that advances your school and adds richness to your programming. That's likely a good fit for the organization. But, if you're approached by an upstart digital software company, pushing incentives for using its virtual school products, that may not align with your school's hands-on model. It may be counterproductive or even detrimental. In any case, your first step is to vet potential partners against the school's mission and vision. The next step is to vet the partnership through the chain of command above you by clearing the relationship with the superintendent or school board.

The second criterion in this measuring stick approach is authenticity. In other words, is the relationship, connection, or action actually going to accomplish what it claims to accomplish? School leaders must learn to say *no* when the potential incentive for a relationship skews the direction of the organization. In other words, you shouldn't reach for the relationship. Unless it's a mandated change, if a new partnership doesn't fit alongside what's already happening, or it seems like it can't deliver on its promise, it's probably too far removed to be of value. You must be intentional about the path forward so you don't overtax the ongoing school culture. To make the point here, let's look at two possible scenarios a school leader might encounter.

> **Makerspace Mania**
>
> A potential donor has been sent your way from a nearby engineering firm. This firm is interested in adopting your school as a sign of support for its local STEM initiatives for children. The partnership would come with a $300,000 investment, and the donors want the money to be used to construct a makerspace and implement a new science curriculum they feel would benefit the school. They would also like to build an enclosed hydroponics gardening center, which would require reducing the footprint of the playground. What are your next steps?

Situations like these require thorough consideration. The prospect of substantial funding is very exciting. That high dollar amount demands that you consider the school's existing programming, and whether this influx of income and programming will add to or detract from what's already in place. If you're in a STEM school and have a staff that would thrive in a makerspace environment, then it's an intriguing idea. It's never quite that simple, though. Keep the following questions in mind when making a decision.

- Will the school board allow for construction? Will we need permits or variances, and who will secure them? Who will manage architectural design and construction?
- Will the board allow a change of curriculum? Does the new science curriculum align with current science expectations and state or province standards?

- Can we afford to give up part of our playground?
- Do we have adequate staffing to run the suggested new programs?
- Does the school community need to be involved in the decision?
- Will we lose this donor if we can't meet all the conditions of the donation?
- Is the donor a negative publicity risk or a positive name in the community?
- Is this level of support likely to continue in the future, or is it a onetime gift?
- Would construction of the makerspace and hydroponics system interfere with the school year?

These are many of the important questions to think through before deciding to engage in this kind of relationship, but let's go back to the idea of measuring sticks. *Mission and vision*: does this concur with the school's mission and vision? *Authenticity*: is it an authentic fit for the school, or is it a reach? Before facing a high-dollar decision like this one, truly knowing your school will help guide the initial decision to move forward with questions and vetting, or to simply say, "Thanks, but not at this time."

> **Teacher's Pet**
>
> Your language arts department head is an avid animal lover. For the past four years, she's brought her beloved pack of rescue dogs into the building during after-school events. Over the years, community members have come to expect the flood of pets at school events and even started bringing in their own. This teacher is the first to your office when you arrive on the job and would like to begin integrating her rescue dogs during the school day to augment her language arts instruction, citing research of dogs' calming, focusing effect on students. She also informs you that she's been talking to the parent-teacher organization about the idea, and they're also very excited by the possibility. Some of the more outspoken parents in their group are even suggesting going to the board to have them consider changing the school mascot to reflect the community's love for dogs. What are your next steps?

Your department chair obviously carries a great deal of weight in the school community, which makes this decision particularly important. Your initial decisions will set precedent, establish ground rules, and define your stance on school culture. They'll also be scrutinized by your staff and parent community. So, before jumping to any quick decision, you have a series of questions to consider in order to gain some clarity on the situation.

- What is the school or district policy on animals in the building? What was the previous administration's stance on animals in school? Perhaps this action was denied in the past, and that's why your teacher has been quick to push the issue, now that there has been administrative turnover. Or perhaps the prior administration made promises of animal inclusion that have now landed in your lap.
- What is the process for changing a mascot? The process may be impossible, which would make your choice easy. Contacting the board or district for clarity will help.
- What is the mood among parents and staff regarding this teacher? Whether the staff member is highly regarded or completely disliked, you'll have context for the impact any decision may have on school culture.
- What is the potential academic impact? What do existing data tell you of this teacher's past performance? If the teacher has struggled academically, adding more distractions to the classroom culture could cause harm.
- What ripple effects might stem from this decision? Will other teachers insist on bringing their pets to school if this is allowed? Are there health, allergen, or air quality issues that may complicate the request?

As illustrated by the bevy of questions surrounding this request, your relationship with this department chair is suddenly pivoting around the issue of pet inclusion. While this isn't what you expected, it is now in your lap and will provide a framework for how you navigate staff suggestions and requests. Remember to ask if this is aligned with the mission and vision, and if this is an authentic fit for the school. On the one hand, if you jump to approve the idea under pressure from both teachers and parents, you may be empowering the relationship, but you risk setting a precedent of allowing parents and teachers to dictate future decision making. On the other hand, if you flat-out deny the request, you set the tone for a "new sheriff in town" culture that could give a negative first impression. In this case, finding some middle ground may be the best course of action. You'll need to foster an ongoing relationship with your staff and parent community, so any choice or action needs to consider that prospect.

To operationalize the ideas we've been discussing, table 3.1 lists some measurements to deliberate and compare when assessing potential partnerships. When assessing potential partnerships, you must weigh the value of the partnership against its impact on the mission. Since some partnerships may necessitate compromise

Table 3.1: Positive and Negative Qualities of Partnerships

Good Partnerships	Questionable Partnerships
Provide ongoing groups of volunteers to help with existing school programs	Offer volunteer help, but with an attempt to push their mission into existing school programs
Provide equipment or clothing for students with no obligations attached	Offer equipment or clothing for students to gain backing for their organization with parents, guardians, or other local influencers
Provide financial compensation for shared brand name recognition	Provide financial compensation to be the exclusive brand name recognized at the school
Provide unrestricted financial donations	Provide financial donations that require strict alignment to the donor's mission
Provide unrestricted retention-incentivizing opportunities and support for staff	Provide retention-incentivizing opportunities and support for staff that require them to serve as perceived employees or spokespeople of the outside organization
Provide training and professional development for existing school programs	Provide training and professional development for additional school programs or curricula that don't enhance the academic or cultural focus of the school
Provide services for ongoing, value-added school projects or physical plant needs	Provide services for new school projects that don't enhance the mission and vision of the school
Provide opportunities for students or staff to safely engage with the community	Provide opportunities for students or staff to engage with the community in a way that could jeopardize safety

(Schwartz, 2016), any partnership's value is measured by the positive or negative contribution to the mission and vision of the organization. A true value-added partnership enhances the mission and vision of both organizations without either partner having to sacrifice its identity to work with the other. A poor partnership may offer tantalizing value at the expense of your school's mission.

New leaders may find themselves feeling trapped if they allow existing questionable partnerships to move forward unchecked. That said, there is no better time to re-establish boundaries and make adjustments than at the beginning of a leadership transition. For you, the new steward of the school, navigating out of risky relationships is an important early task. This is your chance to set your school on the right track—don't be afraid to take it!

Fundraising and Friend-Raising

In this section, we continue our focus on authentic and mission-aligned relationships, while introducing the need for additional financial and public support. It doesn't matter what kind of school you lead; raising funds and building public support are important tasks that need continuous direction from the building leader.

Fundraising

First off, let's discuss fundraising and distinguish between three levels of contributions.

1. Drops in the bucket
2. Midsize contributions
3. Capital campaigns

Drops in the Bucket

Much of school fundraising generates a very small "drop in the bucket" amount of income for the organization. Fundraisers like box-top collection, candle sales, popcorn sales, coupon books, Amazon Smile, and subscription sales are all commonplace. Many of these smaller fundraisers have specific targets like funding the parent-teacher organization, athletics, or other extracurricular programming. These fundraisers have their place but shouldn't be the sole source of fundraising income.

If you've arrived in a new setting and some annual or ongoing fundraisers are already in place, you can vet them for continuation based on the same criteria used for relationships—mission fit and authenticity. If there is a long list of ongoing "drop in the bucket" fundraisers, it may be time to scale back. If there are none, it might be time to activate some focused fundraisers in areas that can support small school-based programs.

Funding fatigue is another factor to consider with smaller fundraisers. You can ruin relationships with your parents and community if you try to sell them chocolates and coupons too often. Schools that push fundraisers every few months fatigue the community, and donations typically taper off. Worse yet, it becomes harder to ask for larger donations if the local community is burned out and no longer willing to support the cause.

Midsize Contributions

Midsize fundraising opportunities—those that fall between popcorn sales and a campaign to fund a new building—can be the most confusing of the three. Typically, these midsize contributions range between $2,000 and $10,000. They often come from corporate donors or philanthropic foundations looking to contribute their income to a worthy cause. They are extremely meaningful and can add tremendous value to the organization. Over the course of a year, these contributions can add up to significant amounts and cover staffing positions or facility and landscape upgrades.

This level of funding is where the school leader (especially in smaller settings) is most involved in deciding whether the opportunity for additional funds will positively impact the school. The corporate and philanthropic world are often motivated by tax write-offs and annual foundation pledges to improve the greater community. If a leader understands this dynamic, he or she can begin to build friendships (and, at the same time, build awareness) so when the need to give to the community arises, the school is in the conversation as a possible recipient.

It's very rare that these midsize funds simply land in your lap. It's even more rare that these funds arrive unrestricted, without any specific allocation. If that happens, you and your organization are extremely lucky. More often, these funds are the result of the school leader's efforts around relationship building, and they are sometimes targeted to specific school uses. We call these efforts *friend-raising*, which we'll discuss in the next section.

Capital Campaigns

A capital campaign is a large fundraising effort that targets funds for a specific reason (often renovation or construction) and is typically limited to a specific amount of time. In the traditional public school setting, any significant high-dollar fundraiser is likely going to be driven by the district. In the charter or private school world, significant fundraisers are usually structured into capital campaigns for physical assets. Whether public or private, larger campaigns can become enormous efforts with clearly defined financial goals but are often run by professional campaign directors or certified fundraising executives.

Friend-Raising

By our definition, *friend-raising* is a patient, proactive, and more meaningful version of fundraising. While capital campaigns and small-dollar fundraisers both utilize the scattered approach of soliciting as many potential donors as possible in hopes that a few will actually contribute, friend-raising is targeted and proactive in building relationships that may lead to future funding. It involves the process of identifying a potential partner, and then taking the time to build relationships and develop trust before asking for financial support. A potential partnership between a school and hospital, for example, may involve months of volunteer visits, collaborative meetings, and sharing of resources. If it's a potential private donor, the friend-raising initiative may involve repeated invitations to help at school or assist with special projects. These experiences allow a school leader the opportunity to identify partnerships that align with the school's mission and vision.

These relationships, when initially built without financial strings, can grow authentically as both sides gain confidence in their mission and vision alignment. Later, after the relationship is established and two authentic partners are working side by side, the friend-raising process can shift into a fundraising relationship. It becomes easier to ask for specific support from the friend or partner who understands the need. Often, the friend or partner will see the need and offer support without being asked. Leaders need to understand that this is the long game of fundraising. It can take a while to develop, but these partners are worth the effort, often circling back to make their financial support an annual gift.

The strongest relationships, funding partnerships, or business friendships are those that become symbiotic. They grow through collaboration and augment the momentum and capacity of both sides. It's still important to assess the value of these relationships, though. While it's altruistic to assume every relationship leads to beneficial symbiotic harmony, it's important to know which endeavors merit an A+ and which deserve an F.

Community Engagement

In this section, we extend the concept of friend-raising into a school's ongoing work with the community. Unlike friend-raising, this kind of work isn't designed to raise money. Rather, it's designed to cement the school's position as a family resource, project partner, and hub of support for the local community. Schools, families, and communities are inextricably connected. Consider this example.

> Teachers and staff at my school are evaluated annually, and each evaluation includes a component of community involvement and external engagement. Our staff are given repeated opportunities to engage with area festivals, fairs, expos, neighborhood cleanups, food drives, clothing drives, and community meetings. These experiences build a depth of

> understanding and trust and tighten the bond between the school and the greater community.
>
> My top administrators are expected to be community participants off site and regular "friendly faces" in the neighborhood. Local organizations and agencies of support should come to count on the school's advocacy and assistance in community-based initiatives. I want all those in our community with or without students in the school to proudly claim our school as their own.

As illustrated in this example, the school leader has a top-down approach to community involvement. The leader has set the tone (from evaluation to collaboration) for school-community engagement. Whether a traditional public, private, or charter school, if you're serving a local population of students, then the community will view your school as a community school. An effective school leader should take that responsibility to heart.

Pause & Reflect

What does it mean to you to be a community school? What community engagement efforts will best serve both your organization and the larger community?

Are there any existing community engagement efforts that could be leveraged for a stronger school-community connection?

A Definition of Community

A school has both an *internal community* and an *external community*. Internal efforts are very important to a school's success, but they only represent one portion of the community. When we only engage with our internal community, it alienates the greater community beyond the school's direct population.

The traditional approach to school-community work has certainly been centered around activating the teacher-parent-student community in a way that builds support and trust in service of the student learning. As Anne T. Henderson (2007) demonstrates in *Beyond the Bake Sale: The Essential Guide to Family-School Partnerships*, students with parents who are actively involved in their education are more likely to earn higher grades and test scores, and then to enroll in higher-level programs. This effect of internal community is well tested and forms the heart of many school initiatives, but it continues to exclude the external community.

In addition to the students, teachers, and staff within a school, the word *community* should apply more broadly. When we talk about external community, we're talking about everyone else in your area who either does not have children or does not send their children to your school. Building additional relationships in the external community is an important practice to expand your spheres of influence beyond the school walls.

As a comparison, think about your own circle of friends. A study conducted in 2015 found that adults tend to have four close support friends and thirteen close offline friends (Dunbar, 2016). Combined with close family, that's your internal community. As a starting point, your external community would include distant relatives, school friends, neighbors, and social media friends. This group is obviously much larger—in social media alone, the average person has 388 connections (Dunbar, 2016). In addition, you have the common places you and your friends interact, like local businesses, places of worship, hospitals, sporting venues, restaurants, gyms, stores, bars, and so on.

As a school leader, think about the many connections you or your staff may have in your external community. Now, think about how you or your staff currently leverage that external community in your day-to-day life. How many routines do you have that revolve around shopping, working out, worship, or entertainment? How many of your social friends do you share information with, coordinate events with, and so on? Those connections, friends, resources, businesses, and opportunities are also at your school's disposal if you're willing to utilize them. Even if you are new to the area, when you factor in the circles of influence of your staff and students' families, the sheer number of opportunities becomes staggering. In other words, it simply isn't good enough to focus on what happens within your property lines (your internal community) when you have access to such a rich position in your external community. The following story suggests the potentially tremendous impact external community relationships can have on your school.

> By my fourth year leading our school, I'd gone from no community partnerships to the following: a free nurse and nursing clinic provided by the nearby hospital; an engineering firm offering volunteers for our robotics teams; free student dinners provided by the local YMCA; free classroom supplies once a week provided by a local advocacy organization; free

> after-school programming provided by a local environmental group; free data disaggregation by a national nonprofit; a community resource officer on call from the local police department; chairs and tables for school events provided by a local church; literally millions of dollars in community-connected funding; and I can go on and on.
>
> But, all of these great perks came at a price. I had to invest years of my time walking alongside these organizations so they understood my vision, trusted me, and believed I was in it for the long haul.

As this example indicates, by connecting with the external community, a school can become an anchor institution.

Schools as Anchor Institutions

Anchor institutions are organizations that provide stabilizing resources for diverse populations and a variety of influencers in a locally defined area (Taylor, McGlynn, & Luter, 2013). In the book *Schools and Urban Revitalization: Rethinking Institutions and Community*, Kelly L. Patterson and Robert Mark Silverman (2014) define anchor institutions and how they revitalize communities: "Where the private sector disinvests from the inner city, public and nonprofit institutions step in and provide engines to economic revitalization and promote greater equity in society" (p. i).

In the United States, educators are beginning to recognize how schools can play the role of anchor, or serve as supportive pillars for the community. Particularly, "inner-city public schools are anchor institutions that are situated in distressed, jobless and underdeveloped neighborhoods. They are rooted in these locales because of their mission, capital investment and clientele" (Taylor et al., 2013, p. 111). In other words, inner-city public schools often become centers for engagement because they're situated in distressed, underemployed, and underdeveloped neighborhoods. Some of these schools have followed the neighborhood journey for decades. Other are more intentionally located there because of their mission or clientele.

Geoffrey Canada, founder of the Harlem Children's Zone, famously connected school and community in the anchor model, saying, "Fix the schools without fixing the families and community, and children will fail; but they will also fail if you improve the surrounding community without fixing the schools" (as cited in Taylor & McGlynn, 2010, p. 33). The organization Democracy Collaborative (n.d.) outlines the need for anchors in a way we find to be very compelling: "Emerging trends related to globalization—such as the decline of manufacturing, the rise of the service sector, and a mounting government fiscal crisis—suggest the growing importance of anchor institutions to local economies." In other words, in a local neighborhood context, the school can play a very positive role as an anchor institution for the community.

So when you ask yourself the question, "What is community engagement?," don't leave out the external component. As we've established, education revolves around relationships and partnerships, and external community engagement is no exception. Finding ways to support local community initiatives beyond the day-to-day operations of the educational process will yield many unforeseen advantages for your organization, as long as you are patient enough to engage in the work. To kick-start the process, we've listed some simple examples of how to begin engaging in anchor work.

1. Offer up the school as a meeting site for neighborhood organizations and community events.
2. Work collaboratively with the local neighborhood to develop an annual celebration.
3. Partner with local community organizations on a joint fundraiser that can be held on school grounds.
4. Offer a safe space for computer and internet access.
5. Work with school nursing staff to make health services available to the community after school hours.
6. Hold neighborhood coffee and doughnut gatherings in the school cafeteria.
7. Participate in neighborhood meetings and cleanup projects.
8. Offer up the school as a location for food bank or clothing bank assistance.

Expectations for teachers and staff around external community engagement will vary depending on the school setting. If your teachers belong to a union that narrowly defines their responsibilities, you may only be able to ask for volunteers. You'll need to build support and buy-in for the mission so that staff and parents are willing to commit their time and energy to greater community initiatives. In an independent school or other nonunion environment, responsibilities beyond the school day may be more acceptable; those responsibilities might even appear in contract expectations, such as supervising students in a community cleanup effort or participating in a neighborhood association meeting or event. In either case, schools that operate exclusive of the local community eventually cause distrust or conflict. On the positive side, when schools form strong connections with the local community, they can leverage additional opportunities for their students, attract additional funding through collaborative community grants, benefit from a great deal of word-of-mouth marketing, and serve as a model for other organizations in the quest for community revitalization and growth.

School leaders should consider identifying and activating people on their teams who are willing to participate in the local community through neighborhood organizations, support organizations, community centers, food banks, festivals, and so on. The school is a natural hub for community interaction, both internal and external. New leaders should make every attempt to provide clear pathways for the school to interact with the community, and to draw in external support for ongoing internal efforts.

Summary

In this chapter, we explored several aspects of relationships in education. Education is a people business—leaders need to understand emotional intelligence and appraise potential partnerships so they can effectively establish relationships, raise funds, and engage with the community. Build a foundation of a strong internal community, but don't get caught up inside your four walls. Successful programs extend beyond individual efforts, and beyond classrooms and the school. Educating your students takes a community of support. Your capacity to build and maintain relationships as part of your leadership will drive positive change in all aspects of your school. In the next chapter, we will discuss managing your school facility and its operations.

Chapter 3 Reflection Questions

1. What systems can you implement to stay focused on your school's mission and vision when stakeholders, organizations, and vendors barrage you as the new leader of the school? How can the relationship measuring sticks help with this process?

2. How might you develop pathways for intentionally building relationships with your staff? Can you come up with three to five such pathways?

3. How can the concept of emotional intelligence influence your personal ability to lead staff?

4. How will you strike a balance between focus on strategic systems and relationship agility in your leadership?

5. How might community engagement invite change or improvement to your specific school setting?

CHAPTER 4
Manage the Operation

One of the most challenging aspects of school leadership is managing the facility and operations of your school. You cannot do everything yourself, but you must maintain control. Nothing drives a leader to career change more than a lack of control over the operation. In a traditional public environment, this can manifest in front office power plays, district micromanagement, or maintenance crews crippling an operation to suit their availability. In charter and private settings, subcontracted service providers, authorizers, board members, and even neighbors can make managing the organization a major headache. Of course, the vast majority of staff members have good intentions—they are just trying to do their jobs. They cannot wait for you to make every decision; they can't sit and do nothing if you're focused on another task or department. Your school will operate no matter what, so it's up to you to stay engaged, manage your team actively, and maintain your leadership role. You may be the school leader, but if you're not in control of your school, then someone else is.

This is simply human nature. It's a group-dynamics process that happens whether we intend it or not. Any setting must have strong, consistent leadership to establish normalcy, set boundaries, and maintain balance. In response to effective, respectful leadership, the group members will perform their roles more cohesively. When there's a void in any given hierarchical situation, someone will step in and fill it. In the world of a school leader, it often plays out like this: if you are unsure about a building repair, someone will step in and tell you how and when it will be repaired. If you're too distracted to design the schedule, someone will step in and do it the way she thinks it should be done. If you're disengaged from janitorial systems, someone will step in and set his own standards for building maintenance. If you appear not to be in control, someone may take advantage or challenge your leadership. In each of those situations, the work being done will still reflect directly back on you.

As a leader, you have to trust and work with your team while also maintaining oversight. Your job is to delegate appropriately and manage continuously. In the following sections, we provide advice for this important leadership task.

> **Pause & Reflect**
> What are the distractions in your day-to-day work that steal your attention and make you indecisive on more important tasks? How can those distractions be mitigated so your focus is more aligned with higher-level matters?

Task Delegation

No leader can perform every task him- or herself. Assigning responsibility for certain operations to your team members is a requirement for successful leadership. At the same time, you cannot simply assign a task to someone and forget about it. Delegation is insufficient; effective leaders employ *managed delegation*. This is an active process that involves three central considerations: (1) deciding which tasks to delegate, (2) managing those delegations, and (3) avoiding complacency.

Deciding What to Delegate

The first step in managed delegation of operational tasks is deciding which you should personally perform and which you should delegate to your team. If a task is critical to the function and well-being of the organization, you should consider taking personal responsibility for that task. But not all tasks are equal. Many mission-related tasks have to be completed, but not all have to have the school leader directly involved. If the task is "busy work" or rote operations, adding only basic support to the organization, you're in a situation where delegating the task is more appropriate. To illustrate, first consider delegating responsibilities that can likely be handled by others, such as the following.

- **Developing meal plans for a special staff luncheon:** While fun, this is a task that clerical staff can perform for you.
- **Planning spaces for after-school programs:** Space planning will impact the school, but this task is better suited for an administrator or staffer who can do the work and report back with suggestions.
- **Performing an analysis aligning lesson plans to academic standards:** It's important to know that teachers' curricula are aligned to standards, but this is arduous work better suited for an academic specialist on your staff who can report back when done.
- **Observing driveline and drop-off to make sure parents aren't waiting too long in their vehicles:** Complaints often arise from

parents due to traffic around the school. But, unless there is a dire emergency, these observations can be assigned to other staff with reporting responsibilities so you can stay informed.

- **Monitoring hallway procedures for efficient transitions:** It's always a good practice to monitor the flow and culture of the school from time to time, but regular ongoing monitoring should be delegated so that your focus can be placed on higher-level issues.

On the other hand, the following examples are situations in which you should consider taking on responsibilities that need your direct attention and influence.

- **Meeting with staff leaders to debrief on the fidelity of the school model:** As school leader, you should meet regularly with your staff leaders. If this duty is delegated or ignored, you risk creating a leadership void and losing touch with the day-to-day realities of teaching and learning in your school.
- **Observing teachers and providing feedback:** It's always a challenge, but great leaders mold and shape classrooms, ensuring the academic model is in place. While it's fine to share responsibility for time-consuming observations, leaders need to know what's happening in the classrooms to be effective evaluators and mentors.
- **Participating in special education case conferences:** Understanding the impact of accommodations and modifications for students with disabilities in your school is critical to the school's success. If these duties are too heavily delegated, the leader may lose touch with the legal requirements for a percentage of the population.
- **Developing frameworks for solidifying the school's academic model:** If this task is delegated, then whoever is in charge has the ability to alter the basic academic frameworks of the school. Model-specific work should be performed by the school leader.
- **Meeting with parents on challenging discipline issues:** As tension rises in disciplinary issues, the school leader needs to be involved. Many staff below the leadership level may struggle to meet the needs of a parent dealing with tense, complicated issues. Delegating these situations away may cause them to escalate.

Task management is a trap that catches many leaders. As the top authority figure in the building, you may feel compelled to own all problems, especially the ones you have the experience and expertise to solve. This is a common issue, as leaders often gravitate to what they're good at rather than to what is most important to the organization in that moment. Because they're comfortable working within their knowledge base and ability, leaders can get caught with an overwhelming list of procedural tasks, with no bandwidth left for mission-critical tasks. This situation can entrap school leaders: if they aren't careful, critical tasks can get delegated to other staff with less ability and experience, or those who do not have the authority to make key decisions. This could be the beginning of the end for many leaders, and it can happen without anyone realizing how the downward spiral began. Simply put, leaders can get caught in a comfort zone of tasks they feel more capable of completing rather than making choices based on the priority of the tasks. Evaluating tasks against their importance to the organization and their appropriateness for delegation will help avoid this trap. Once you've delegated tasks appropriately, you're ready to begin managing those delegations.

Managing Delegated Tasks

Program and building operations will certainly involve many tasks that you'll need to delegate. In many cases, the staff members who take responsibility for these duties may be more knowledgeable about their tasks than you are. To be successful, you must acknowledge what you understand and mindfully accept what you don't know. Along with this, you must be aware of the leadership void you create when you delegate or offload any responsibility. In other words, when you remove yourself from the perceived authority of that task, others might assume there is a shift in authority, or a lack of leadership in the process. To protect your system from this perception, you have to be committed to managing your delegations.

The keys to managing tasks for which you are not directly responsible are *timelines* and *measurable results*. For instance, if you hand off food service to the district or to a subcontractor, schedule a monthly meeting (timelines) to guarantee you understand the program, track progress (measurable results), and maintain the authority to approve any necessary changes. If you delegate school-based state reporting, specify that you need to review each report a certain number of days prior to submission (timelines) and create a simple tool for tracking submissions (measurable results).

Timelines and measurable results make managing delegated tasks much more concrete and actionable. Every leader delegates, but many fail to follow up. Following up can be as simple as saying, "I'd like you to have that done by Monday at 8 a.m., and then run it past me. Thanks!" In that example, the timeline is the Monday deadline, and the measurable result is the review to verify completion. This small tweak to your operational style puts you in charge without forcing you to personally complete every single task.

Even the most basic tasks assigned from a leader to a staff member will present opportunities for timelines and measurable results. Consider the following email reminder examples from a school leader to an academic dean.

Version 1: "Mr. Tyser, I want to remind you that some of our teachers did not submit their lesson plans on time. You know this shouldn't happen . . ."

Version 2: "Mr. Tyser, I've noticed that three of our teachers missed the last two lesson plan deadlines. Please work with staff to make sure all of this week's lesson plans are submitted by close of business tomorrow, and next week's plans are done by close of business Friday."

In version 2, it is obvious there is a system of recording lesson plan submissions (measurable result). When combined with the direct time-based request for submission, there is little confusion as to who is in charge and how the task should be interpreted. It may seem rudimentary, but these are small checks and balances that maintain your leadership and prevent your operations from going off the rails.

Avoiding Complacency

Even with timelines and measurable results in place, it can be challenging to stay on top of all your managed delegations. Our environments can apply stress and pressures that impede our focus and our intentions until we're prioritizing backwards and delegating away our authority. This is what happens when you concentrate too heavily on the tasks that feel the most comfortable. Completing the comfortable tasks makes it seem like you're on the right track without perceiving a negative shift—other key portions of the system left neglected—until too late. Good leaders create checks and balances for this issue, understanding that perception is easily flawed. Consider the following side-by-side task delegation method for checking and balancing your delegated tasks.

Step 1: Make a list of your top ten (or more) most enjoyable tasks that you do for your job.

Step 2: Make another list of your top ten (or more) least favorite tasks that you do for your job.

Step 3: Now look at both lists and circle the tasks that are the most important tasks for the success of the organization. School leaders will often find that there are circled tasks on both lists and, more importantly, uncircled tasks on the list of tasks they enjoy the most.

Step 4:   Now make a new list of the circled tasks, and another new list of all other tasks. The new list of circled tasks represents a great starting point for the tasks the leader should take on personally. The list of remaining tasks includes the ones that can be considered for delegation.

This side-by-side list method isn't a perfect tool for delegation, but it's a great first step for organizing workloads, and bringing to light how easily we slip into the trap of wanting only to do what we like to do. Put simply, this is a flaw in perception that lets us down if we don't pay close attention. We all have flaws, and perceptual flaws can hide critical errors. They represent a tricky component in leadership.

As an example of flawed perceptions, consider the act of seeing, which can demonstrate how our minds often play tricks on us. We've all lost items like our keys, wallet, or phone and frantically searched all over the house to find them. Then, mysteriously, the lost item appears in a place we've already looked. Somehow, we just missed seeing it the first time around. This conundrum is actually rooted in a concept called *change blindness*. Our eyes scan rapidly in moments of change as they map out the details in the world around us. Within this rapid scan period, they are actually unable to provide real-time visual input to the brain, creating lapses with no sight. During these lapses, the brain fills in the gaps with what it thinks should be there. Sometimes, this process leads to errors in visual accuracy, like when your eyes overlook your keys and your brain fills in an image of the kitchen counter from a memory when your keys weren't there (Schutz, Kerzel, & Suoto, 2014). We mention flaws in our visual perception to illustrate how our brains make mistakes and fill in information without us knowing. To further highlight automaticity in mental processes, consider the following story.

> I once struck up a conversation with a stranger named Chris, and we ended up discussing many different ways our brains play tricks on us. Since we were in a restaurant, the conversation began with the idea that the greatest drinks or greatest foods weren't just our favorites because the recipe was so perfect—they were also great because the setting and the company made the memory of the taste better than the taste itself. The memory of the experience inflates our memory of the taste to such an extent that we feel unable to re-create the taste in a different setting.
>
> Chris then brought up our lack of attention to detail while driving, especially when traveling to a familiar place. I added the fact that if you think back on a recent drive and try to remember the turns you made,

> the exits you used, or the times you caught a bad light, you'll struggle to remember the details. Add a cell phone conversation and you're practically on autopilot. In that situation, your mental focus is everywhere except for where it needs to be.
>
> Finally, Chris made the connection to learning, explaining a tactic he used in school of studying the same topic in multiple locations. Knowing that the mind needs variety, he said that when you move to a new place, your mind has to open up and absorb the new space, new conditions, smells, visuals, and so on. This activates the learning process and ties the content memory of what you're studying to multiple places or experiences, locking it in better for future use. Unexpectedly, this conversation with a random stranger provided a great deal of insight into the strangeness of brain function!

These common examples serve as a gateway for accepting lapses in other mental processes, like not realizing you've become too comfortable and lost your focus on proper task management. We're all faulty to a degree, and we all have tendencies to lapse into our comfort zone by focusing on the things we like to do rather than the things we should be doing. To combat this, it's important to recognize our flaws and work to counteract them. Without some sort of prompt or push to step out of your comfort zone (like creating side-by-side lists to stay focused on critical tasks), important tasks are at risk for being handled poorly. This idea is not a new one to managerial science and is connected to what is now called the Yerkes-Dodson Law (Corbett, 2015). This law is based on a 1908 study in which mice learned a habit more quickly when subjected to a moderate electric shock than when subjected to a weak or strong shock (Yerkes & Dodson, 1908). To this same effect, we need to operate with *optimal anxiety*, which is a state of elevated stimulus that actually increases productivity and memory (Lee & Fernandez, 2017). While too much stress can overwhelm us, and too little can leave us underperforming, an optimal level of stimulus enables us (and mice) to perform at our best. Additional effort or stimulus is often needed to improve regular work performance. When we stick to our comfort zone, we risk a drop-off in stimulus or arousal, and we can become apathetic and less productive.

We must continually self-assess, check, and compensate for our own counterproductive tendencies and mental errors to make sure we haven't missed something. Keywords or phrases posted on your wall or placed on your desktop can help you remember to stay the proper course. Completing the side-by-side task list strategy will help you remember to keep the focus on the critical tasks. Even creating a pie chart for your critical daily tasks can help you get past any unnecessary slide into your comfort zone.

To recap the process of managed delegation, recall that if you're not in control of your school, then someone else is. Following that idea, remember to remain committed to managing delegations when you do hand over responsibility. Lastly, we should remain aware that we're all flawed, and work to avoid the tendency to navigate to what we're good at rather than what we should be doing. Those three ideas together create a powerful thought practice for leadership.

> **Pause & Reflect**
>
> Think back. How have you governed what to take on and what to delegate? Do you sometimes lose sight of your delegation-management process?

In the following sections, we explore specific types of tasks that contribute to the operation of a school and how you might delegate and manage them. Specifically, we'll cover managed services (such as technology, facilities management, and subcontractors), emergency planning, and asset inventory.

Managed Services

For your school to function smoothly, a complex web of services, programs, and operations must align and work cohesively. As stated previously, it's such a big job that you can't do it alone: we recommend that someone else at your school oversee facility operations. Yes, there will be times when you need to step in and oversee critical problems, but the day-to-day grind of facility management should fall on the shoulders of an operations manager. This could be a full-time staff member on your administrative team, your assistant principal, your office manager, or even a savvy volunteer. The point is that you need someone you can trust to take some of the time-consuming but important task management off your plate. However, don't just delegate away what you don't know—delegate what you know can be passed on without harming the mission-driven focus of your daily routine. When the operations manager or operations team is ready to take on the ownership of managing all facilities and operations tasks, be sure to schedule regular check-in meetings to keep an eye on the management of this critical department.

It's simply impossible, though, to delegate and manage appropriately if you don't understand the details and importance of all your managed services. There are three categories of managed services for schools: (1) technology, (2) facilities management, and (3) other service providers. We discuss each one to enhance your understanding of its impact on the school operation.

Technology

The importance of functional school technology has increased. In 2010, the United States saw its first official draft of the National Education Technology Plan (NETP; Dede, 2010). Within five years of NETP, a majority of states had begun to mandate digital testing (EdTech Strategies, 2015). Unfortunately, this pressure to modernize education through technology creates a myriad of challenges for school leaders. Access to technology and the internet are the most obvious initial hurdles, especially in underfunded schools in impoverished areas (Fortner, Normore, & Brooks, 2019).

Technology creates ongoing site-based economic difficulties. Limited funding can quickly force the district or school leader to compromise or make concessions that deny certain grades tech access or require sharing a smaller common set of equipment. Let's consider some hypothetical initial costs. The baseline cost of a cheap notebook computer is about $300; a top-end model would be $1,000 per device. If a school has five hundred students, it would cost between $150,000 and $500,000 to outfit the student population with one-to-one devices. Add another thirty-five or forty devices for staff, and this price range increases to $155,000–$545,000. That number only covers one-to-one devices; next, you have to keep in mind classroom instructional technology, such as document cameras, projection or smart whiteboard systems, and so on. The costs on these setups are highly individualized but can quickly run as much as $15,000 per classroom.

These user devices are relatively simple. The hard part of implementing those devices is making sure there is infrastructure to support them. All devices will need a Wi-Fi network. This network will need multiple wireless access points wired back to the switch and spaced evenly around the school to provide a strong enough signal, and broad enough throughput for all devices to work simultaneously. Supporting those access points, you'll need a server (probably two), switch (probably two), filter, and router. The cost of these physical items supporting your network will range wildly between $20,000 and $100,000 depending on your location and purchasing savvy. Installation and setup will cost another $5,000 to $15,000. You'll also need to consider physical infrastructure for storing the end-user devices in each classroom.

Will you need storage carts in each room, power centers, additional outlets, or shelving? Those costs can be as high as $10,000 per classroom.

In addition to devices and infrastructure, you'll need someone to manage all your technology and make sure it's running correctly. Most traditional public schools will utilize an off-site managed services model where a technician logs into the system from a distance to manage the server and work on individual device issues remotely. Remote service lowers costs but may increase frustrations, as it can take longer for a technician to solve a problem remotely. Some off-site managed service models utilize a "technician on call" program so someone can be on site as needed. This can be a workable solution, but typically comes at a higher price. The other option is to employ a full-time, on-site technology specialist who manages everything and fixes problems as they arise. This is usually the most expensive option, but it can go a long way in terms of staff happiness and system efficiency. However, you'll still need a backup plan for when the specialist takes a sick day or is unable to solve a complicated problem. In terms of pricing, remote managed service contracts can be as low as a base teacher salary, and site-based tech scenarios with a high-quality emergency backup plan can cost more than your own salary as the school's leader. The option you choose will depend on your situational needs and constraints. Then, you also have to determine whether you'll manage technology directly or delegate it (with timelines and measurable results) to someone on your team.

Most large districts will handle all managed service costs and make choices for the school in terms of what kind of service best suits the district. Similarly, if a leader is stepping into a building with existing technology and infrastructure, then the challenge of selecting the right contract and right technology has already been dealt with. In a brand-new school, or a private or charter school considering new technology purchases, the school leader (often along with the board) typically has more local control, requiring a bit more industry savvy. For those situations, consider that, in the United States, the national average income per student is hovering near $13,000 (Cornman, Zhou, Howell, & Young, 2018). In 2019, the Australian Curriculum, Assessment and Reporting Authority lists an average income per student for state and territory government funding at $17,531. Whether we're comparing global numbers or state numbers, it's critical to understand your per-student revenue. Thus, for the U.S. school of five hundred students mentioned previously, annual student revenue will bring in roughly $6.5 million. Based on our earlier calculations, this means that school technology costs could approach 10 percent of total student revenue. Spending 10 percent of revenue on technology is simply too much; 3 to 5 percent is a much safer range. No matter your setting, this is a useful criterion for the affordability of technology program expenses.

Facilities Management

The maintenance of your building and grounds is one of the most important aspects of school operations. It goes almost without saying that you'll want to delegate these tasks to your janitorial and maintenance staff and manage them indirectly. This is an easy area to disengage from, but consider the following legend surrounding the construction of St. Paul's Cathedral in England.

> Christopher Wren, one of the great English architects, went out one day to observe the workers building St. Paul's Cathedral, which he had designed. The builders did not recognize him, so he asked a group of three men, "What are you doing?" The first worker responded, "I'm cutting a piece of stone." The second worker replied, "I'm earning five shillings, two pence a day." Finally, the third worker said, "I'm helping Sir Christopher Wren build a beautiful cathedral."

As a more recent example, we can think back to a well-known story about President John F. Kennedy (Nemo, 2014).

> In 1962, President John F. Kennedy visited the National Aeronautics and Space Administration (NASA) to check on the progress of the Apollo space program. During the visit, he noticed a man carrying a broom—a janitor who worked cleaning NASA's facilities. Kennedy interrupted his tour, approached the man, and the following short conversation unfolded.
>
> **JFK:** "Hi, I'm Jack Kennedy. What are you doing?"
>
> **Janitor:** "Well, Mr. President, I'm helping put a man on the moon."

If we apply these stories to a school, we can understand that there are more aspects to janitorial and maintenance than just cleaning and fixing. Those who perform these tasks need to understand, feel part of, and have buy-in for the mission of the organization. If they believe their work benefits the entire organization (like the NASA janitor or the last worker in the Christopher Wren story), their work ethic will serve the organization's mission. If you don't make the effort to include janitors, maintenance workers, and other nonteaching staff as community members, you'll risk creating problems in the facility that distract from and reduce your mission-critical productivity.

Your facilities team has likely been selected for you. Charter and private schools may use a subcontracted service provider. In traditional public schools, the selection process might be coordinated by the district, and the decision makers may or may not know your building well. This does not mean you can't generate buy-in for your program. Remember, this crew is taking over a major task in your domain. Schedule regular meetings with these individuals to establish rapport and manage your delegation. Invite them to staff meetings. Invite them to participate in school events. Have your classes make cards for them on special occasions.

In the following sections, we discuss four key elements of facilities management: (1) janitorial, (2) maintenance, (3) landscaping and snow services, and (4) building security.

Janitorial

Janitorial staff are essential members of any school community. However, too many leaders are unsure of what their janitors do on a regular basis. It's not uncommon that school leaders interact with their janitorial crews primarily when they need someone to clean up sudden emergencies like vomit, spills, toilet backups, or other messes. Of course, this isn't how it should be—you need to actively manage this area, just as you would any task you've delegated.

Begin the year with a detailed walkthrough of the facility with the entire crew (refer to the appendix, page 178, for resources to guide this activity). During that walkthrough, you can collaboratively develop a checklist of daily, weekly, and monthly items for maintenance and cleaning. Give crew members a printed copy of the list for future reference. Then, follow up with quarterly walkthroughs to ensure each item is being maintained appropriately and find out if your janitorial team has sufficient resources. This is effective management and establishes regular communication with your facilities team.

In addition to a specific checklist, we recommend establishing janitorial priorities for your building, aligned with the school's mission and vision. A typical list of priorities will appear in the following order.

1. Classrooms are clean and sanitary.
2. Bathrooms are clean and function properly.
3. The cafeteria is maintained throughout meal service.

4. The entrance to the school is clean, tidy, and professional.
5. Everything else is attended to as needed.

In other words, the academic environment of the classroom is sacred, as are the supporting areas of the school that keep students healthy and happy so they can learn. Janitorial staff must be prepared to do everything with that mindset. You want your crew to say to others, "Our job is to help students learn, and to set our students up for success in the future."

Over time, work on building a relationship with your janitorial staff. Respectful relationships with these team members will help create buy-in for the school mission and vision, thereby increasing work quality, as would be true with any other staff. A positive foundation also makes it easier to address any deficiencies in the maintenance of the school. These team members often do difficult work for relatively low pay; whether you're working with longtime employees or looking to subcontract a new company, the relationships you build with your janitorial staff will make a real difference in their commitment to the mission of the school and consequently the status of your building.

In addition to janitorial staff, it's important to pay attention to cleaning supplies. Many districts purchase and store these supplies at the district level, but that's not always the case. When that responsibility falls to you as the school leader, you'll need to make decisions regarding which supplies to purchase with consideration of their cost. Contracted crews often purchase their own supplies and charge the school or include supplies in their contracts. Look into this prior to contracting, bearing in mind that it's never too late to renegotiate. You'll want to consider a few simple questions: Are the cleaning supplies nontoxic? Ecofriendly? Too expensive? Where are they stored? Who tracks, orders, and buys them when they run low? Can the school save money by purchasing similar supplies for the crew? Typically, school-specific purchasing consortiums can beat the prices janitorial companies charge for supplies. This also allows a school to purchase supplies that are guaranteed to be safe for use around children.

Maintenance

Building maintenance teams are another subset of facilities management that can either be your lifeline or cause some headaches, depending on quality, timeliness, and relationship. The first step in this area is to know who maintains the various elements of your building and whom to call during critical situations. For instance, if the plumbing goes down for more than an hour, you're likely closing school. If a pipe bursts, you're likely closing school. If the power keeps going out, you're likely closing school. Therefore, the people you have on call for solving these kinds of problems are critical to your success. The appendix includes a contact sheet (page 181) for your facilities maintenance professionals, which you can fill out and keep on hand for emergencies.

The complication in this area is that while you (hopefully) only need your maintenance professionals sporadically, when you do need them, it's often urgent. The inference here is to not take them for granted. While they likely reside off-site, you need to have a positive relationship with them for when a maintenance emergency turns your life upside down. The trick to building these relationships is in the smaller maintenance needs. You may have a drippy faucet, leaking water fountain, faulty light switch, tricky lock, torn carpet, or minor wall repair. These accumulate into nonemergency maintenance calls that typically ask contractors or crew members to come out when their schedule allows. During these low-stress visits, you have a great opportunity to connect with individual workers and express your gratitude. Engage in conversation and get to know them as people. Verbal thanks, cards from classes, invitations to lunch or school events, and follow-up thank-you cards or emails can go a long way.

Landscaping and Snow Services

Landscape is another area that new leaders are typically not prepared to manage. Again, larger traditional public schools usually cover this at the district level. There will be a landscape maintenance plan in effect that will have a rotation of properties to be managed over a very structured annual calendar. This doesn't mean that the school leader should ignore this area. If the rotation for mowing the grass is once every two weeks and you live in a rainy part of the country, you're likely getting fairly weedy by day fourteen—and romping about in high weeds and grass is not the best for your students. Don't be afraid to voice concerns to the district maintenance team. No two properties are alike, and the district manager in this department may not be aware of your specific needs.

In settings where the school leader has more autonomy (usually private and charter schools, as well as some public schools in small towns), decisions as to when and how the landscape is managed usually fall directly on the principals. The initial impression given by a school and property is an external one. That means if the landscape and building facade look shabby, then first impressions will trend that direction. Making this more mission-critical is the fact that private and charter schools have to attract their enrollment more purposefully than larger public schools or districts.

An attentively cared-for building on well-manicured grounds can be an important marketing tool.

We recommend setting tangible benchmarks for landscaping to guide conversations around frequency of service. Many larger cities have codes stipulating a specific maximum growth height weeds and grasses must not exceed, after which point a property can be fined for poor upkeep. Individual cities have specific thresholds for this, but as a leader you will need to set an appropriate benchmark based on your school setting. As with janitorial and maintenance staff, a comprehensive walk-through with your landscaping crew and intentional relationship building can go a long way in establishing managed delegation in this area.

Bad weather also presents facilities challenges for your school. If you live in an area with snow and ice, you'll need a plan for clearing sidewalks, parking lots, and driveways. In a traditional public school, the district may send out a team at a given time (perhaps 5 or 6 a.m.) to clear your lot and sidewalks. In a charter or private setting, you'll negotiate these expectations when you contract with that particular service provider. Note that most summer landscaping companies also provide snow-and-ice service in the winter, so you may be able to use one company for both, thereby saving time and money.

In all situations, snow-and-ice services are usually initiated at a certain accumulation level. In other words, your contract may state that you'll receive services if snow exceeds two inches or ice accumulates to more than a tenth of an inch. These levels are typically negotiable, but lower levels mean more frequent service and higher costs. As a school leader, you'll need to know that level because you are responsible for clearing any snow or ice below that cutoff. That can be a source of pain when it catches you by surprise.

Building Security

Concerns about building security are an unfortunate reality. The duties of monitoring the security system, properly training staff on security protocols, and showing up for security calls at any hour of the day or night often fall on the school leader. As a portion of preservice training, leaders should make sure every staff member is clearly trained on use of the school's security system to access and depart the building outside of regular work hours. Alarm systems can intimidate teachers into mistakes and avoidance, so the quality of this training will directly contribute to the security of the building.

In larger settings, the school may have a security or resource officer. The largest schools may even have their own police department. Again, establishing a positive relationship with the members of your security team will yield better results. You have entrusted them with the responsibility of keeping the facility safe. Manage that delegation with checklists (see the appendix, page 178), walkthroughs, and goodwill, and your security detail will treat the school with a more vested interest.

If your building has a camera system for security, make sure you have access to view the footage. Whether you handle monitoring or recording when incidents arise or you delegate the task, you'll want to know how to access the system on your own. Learn how to log in, view, and search by date, time, and camera. Sometimes, a quick review of tape can help clarify urgent situations and enable you to make the best possible decision. You want to be in a position to check the footage even if the primary security personnel are not available.

Other Service Providers

While technology and facilities management are two significant areas, there are many other school operations that you'll likely delegate to professional service providers. This chapter is starting to accumulate many checklists, walkthroughs, and negotiations. By now, it should be obvious that managing the facility can be a full-time job all on its own, as we suggested at the beginning of this section (page 70).

The following sections detail essential concerns and attendant tasks prior to opening the doors in the new academic year. Larger public school districts take care of many of these for their leaders, but charter and private leaders may need to manage these on their own.

Air Quality, Water Quality, and Plumbing Inspections

Legal standards are very strict about air quality in schools. However, school air quality audits are rare, and they typically only happen if someone reports the school for poor air quality. If you fail an audit, you'll likely be fighting some immediate and expensive mandates to improve your airflow or HVAC systems. These kinds of extensive upgrades can get very costly, so it's best to monitor your own air quality and make smaller, more frequent upgrades as needed.

While there are water sanitation and hygiene (WASH) standards globally (Wagner & Samuelsson, 2019), as of 2019, there is no federal mandate in the United States for water quality testing in existing schools (U.S. Environmental Protection Agency, 2019). New schools are required in most states to prove their water quality is safe. However, a good leader will monitor this important aspect of health and safety regardless of outside requirements. Water quality tests are very inexpensive, and some local and state initiatives pay for testing, so it's worth talking to your city representatives to find a funding source. If a test finds that the school has bad water quality (heavy metals or particles of undesirable elements), it needs to be addressed immediately. Stand up for your community in these situations, and don't be afraid to publicize the issue: students' health and safety is paramount.

On a related note, plumbing is another critical area for the facility. Plumbing inspections are not always required for schools, but working bathrooms are more important than most leaders realize. If the bathrooms are nonfunctional, the school must close. Leaders (or operations managers) can do themselves a favor by checking the plumbing history of the building. A quick call to the plumbing vendor for the site will allow for a review of past visits, repairs, prices, and so on. If there is a long history of backed-up drains and sewer failures, at least you'll be aware of the potential for issues. Proactive annual inspections or drain clearing can keep the pipes functional for the remainder of the year.

Food Service Inspections

Food service inspections by the health department are usually quarterly occurrences. They might be scheduled or be a surprise visit. Regardless of whether you're informed in advance or not, you and your cafeteria staff need to be prepared to meet the inspection team four times annually. As a school leader, you're not required to know the details of food service, but you should get to your kitchen and keep an eye out for some basic elements of cleanliness and quality. The following twelve points will give you a good idea of whether you're likely to pass food service inspections.

1. Does the kitchen look clean? Would you feel comfortable serving or eating food prepared on the surfaces?
2. Is the dry food stored off the floor in a separate area?
3. Is the food in the cold storage dated and labeled?
4. Is there ample room for washing dishes, with a hand-washing area separate from the dishwashing area?
5. Do all faucets work?
6. Does all equipment power on?
7. Do the freezers have working temperature gauges? Are they below zero degrees Fahrenheit?

8. Do the refrigerators have working temperature gauges? Are they above freezing but below forty degrees?
9. Are the ceiling vents and stove vent hoods clean?
10. Are the walls a single, light color with a cleanable surface?
11. Is there a cleaning schedule for the area?
12. Do the food warmers have a temperature sensor? If not, are they tracked for temperature throughout food service?

There is much more to running a high-quality kitchen, but this list will help you stay informed about food service even though you've delegated responsibility to your cafeteria staff. If you notice shortcomings in any of these twelve items, you'll want to communicate the problem and follow up to ensure the lapse in quality is overcome.

Playground Inspections

Safe playground equipment is a major concern for any type of school. Equipment used for playgrounds is specially designed and must be thoroughly tested and approved for use by schools. This kind of vetted equipment comes at a different price point, and from vendors who have a proven track record of providing safe school equipment. If you need to purchase new playground equipment, it will be a major budget consideration. Should you be lucky enough to have existing equipment, then your job is to make sure it's kept in good repair. Either way, the playground must have an annual inspection. If not coordinated by the district, your city's code enforcement team will be able to tell you who provides these inspections. You'll need to schedule this inspection sixty days prior to school opening so that you have ample time to complete the inspection and make any requested improvements prior to opening day.

Fire Safety Inspections

Mandatory fire safety inspections by the local fire marshal usually cover the physical building (occupancy limits, exits, and so on), fire alarms, suppression systems, and emergency plans. Inspections must be completed annually and on file before school starts. If you find yourself heading into the start of the year without having had a fire inspection, give your fire alarm company a call. Luckily, fire incidents have seriously declined over the years due to improved fire safety, but that does not mean we can stop maintaining the systems that have contributed to that decline. Have your facilities, alarms, and fire suppression systems inspected early in the summer to avoid unnecessary hassles or delays prior to opening.

Emergency Planning and Crisis Management

Every school must have an emergency planning document on file internally. Because this document reveals how a school reacts in a crisis, this is not a public document, but it is critical to local crisis response. Such a document typically includes fire drill exit routes, lockdown procedures, active shooter procedures, bomb threat procedures, communications and media guidelines, evacuation sites, severe weather procedures, and so on. This document needs to be updated annually, reviewed with staff, and kept in multiple secure locations on site. Typically, this document is also shared with local law enforcement. If you work in a district or network, be sure to collaborate with your district or network security team to develop your emergency plan procedures and to train your staff for potential emergencies. In a private or charter school, there is likely a plan on file, so you'll want to locate it and make sure it's up to date. If you are opening a new school, this plan will need to be put together prior to opening day.

Asset Inventory

It is essential as a leader to know what resources you have at your disposal. While some organizations may require an asset inventory, few actually do it (or do it well). Most schools operate without one, and what happens as a result typically goes along similar lines as in the following stories.

> **Wayward Workbooks**
>
> Jerry was a K–5 school principal. It was nearly time for state testing, and his fifth-grade lead teacher ran into his office in a panic letting him know two more students had lost their workbooks. The grade had already been sharing. Now they'd be working three students to a workbook, and learning would slow to a crawl.
>
> Jerry promised to take care of things and calmly sent his teacher back to class. After stopping everything to call around, he finally got through to the company representative and negotiated twenty workbooks to be rushed to the school via drop shipment from the warehouse, arriving one week later. The workbooks and rush shipping came to $2,700.
>
> That summer, Jerry was looking for some past enrollment forms in storage and came across an unopened box of brand-new fifth-grade workbooks. The school had had them all along and didn't even know it. Learning had suffered, the classroom instruction had suffered, and the budget took a hit—all from not having a good inventory on hand.

> **The Damaged Door**
>
> Sherisse was an operations manager at a large international private school. The school had been operating for more than fifty years, but she had only been in her position for the past year. A classroom door had been damaged beyond repair, and the school's headmaster had tasked her with "repairing or replacing the door ASAP."
>
> Sherisse went to work, calling everyone from woodworkers to manufacturing companies. She found out quickly that the door was solid-core oak, with an irregular window and of an irregular size. It couldn't be repaired because of damage to the hinge attachment and cracks along the grain. A replacement would need to be custom made, and was quoted at $1,200 plus shipping, with delivery in four to six weeks.
>
> For the next six weeks, the school placed stanchions in front of the classroom door at night to try and keep evening visitors out of the classroom. On the very day the new door arrived, Sherisse was tracking down a leak in the basement utility room when she came across two extra classroom doors stacked against the wall. She'd be prepared for the next time she had a door incident but had just spent $1,200 and six weeks solving a problem that could have been fixed for free in one day, had she only known she already had replacement doors.

As these examples demonstrate, you should inventory your resources even if it's not required. Count and record everything in the school that isn't quickly consumable—every chair, table, computer, cable, lamp, cart, cabinet, shelf, trash can, book, picture, desk, and so on. It's a constant time and money saver to know what you actually have on hand.

The initial work to create an inventory can be a tall task, but all the heavy lifting comes up front. If updated annually, it's easy work each summer. Annual updates only deal with attrition (what broke or was moved out of the school) and replacement (what was added or upgraded).

Summary

This chapter provided a comprehensive look at what it takes to manage the operation of your school. Learning to delegate tasks while still actively managing those delegations is key to successful leadership. You can't do everything yourself, but you must maintain awareness of and authority over every aspect of the school. Some of the tasks you might delegate to professional service providers include technology, facilities management, and safety inspections. We also covered emergency planning and asset inventories. In the next chapter, we move to more student-centered topics and discuss schoolwide behavior management.

Chapter 4 Reflection Questions

1. How will the concept of managed delegation impact your leadership in your school setting?

2. What concrete steps can you take to proactively regulate your task list, incorporating both organizational priority and optimal anxiety to be sure you delegate your needs in an efficient and effective manner?

3. In what ways can you intentionally manage services like janitorial, landscaping, and so on?

4. How prepared are you in the school security arena? What steps will you take to ensure a safe and orderly environment for students and staff?

5. Review operational tasks to be completed prior to the start of the school year. How will you ensure these are completed before school begins? Which tasks will you complete, and which will you delegate? To whom will each task be delegated?

Lead From the Start © 2020 Solution Tree Press • SolutionTree.com
Visit **go.SolutionTree.com/leadership** to download this free reproducible.

CHAPTER 5

Codify Schoolwide Norms

In the case of many lifesaving practices and tools like the Heimlich maneuver, cardiopulmonary resuscitation, automated external defibrillators, or epinephrine auto-injectors, we find that there are explicit instructions and step-by-step training. After all, if you are saving someone's life, that critical task should be clearly defined and the knowledge universally understood. While the process of education in our schools may not be as immediately critical in a single moment as a lifesaving procedure, it still involves the lives of our youth and thus deserves similar structure and clarity. In this chapter, we'll discuss norms and procedures that will help you create a stable school environment that is conducive to student learning.

Establishing Norms

Without clearly defined structure, your school culture can be left to interpretation and can become inconsistent from classroom to classroom. Norms (normalized procedures and expectations) set standards for how everything works in a way that can be understood by all. The day-to-day operations of a school involve countless processes. Things like lesson plans, instructional design, discipline, bathroom passes, hall procedures, recess, lunch, classroom management, assemblies, office protocol, and parent communication are all facets of the school culture that can be regularized with clear, concise expectations.

While there are many different school programs that focus on norms (Positive Behavioral Interventions and Supports [PBIS], for example), schools can create norms regardless of whether they've implemented one of these specific initiatives. The easiest first step in norming is the utilization of a common language. Wherever students, staff, and parents go in the building, there are opportunities for common language. The following list provides a good start for setting up common language in a school.

- Label halls and rooms so they are all referenced in the same manner.
- Develop and post schoolwide behavioral language for use in every classroom, regardless of grade.
- Develop and post student character traits (a list of three to five is ideal) to prioritize in every classroom, regardless of grade.
- Create common disciplinary forms for all age and grade levels.
- Create common hall passes and nurse passes for all grades.
- Post hallway expectations with identical language for all halls so that staff use the same language with all students.
- Develop common language for academic data (growth, targets, testing, grade point average [GPA], homework, and so on) when working with staff across grade levels.
- Post the school mission and vision and be sure all staff know them.
- Use the same template and formatting for all school-parent communication. Standardize the font and type size used in all official school communication.
- Create sample scripts for common phone calls home (attendance, discipline, sports, and so on) to help teachers communicate consistently.

Visit **go.SolutionTree.com/leadership** to download a free reproducible version of this checklist.

These simple activities establish a cultural foundation and prevent a great deal of confusion. We suggest using a list like this as a base from which you and your administrative team can develop your own inventory of essential communication norms. As you talk through each item on the list, you'll find your team coming up with additional items specific to your system.

Even though these lists are concrete and easy to understand, instituting a common language takes time and effort. It can be difficult to get an entire staff of different personalities and different tendencies to communicate the same way, but it's worth the effort. Once a team begins to lock in and adhere to communication norms, other areas (like recess expectations, lunchroom procedures, professional development, interpersonal communication, and so on) tend to fall in line.

> **Pause & Reflect**
>
> How structured are the current systems in your school? What systems for norms are already in place? Can your leadership structure support a more cohesive set of norms?

Positive Norms

Throughout the rest of this chapter, we have much to say about norming the negative aspects of culture; that is, how to prevent misbehavior and respond when students do not meet expectations. However, schools need positive norms, too. If your system is nothing but endless policy on what to do when students do something wrong, you'll be chasing the tail of the problem forever. You need to build a culture of positivity for students to emulate. There are many predesigned models, such as character education programs, that come ready-made for positive high expectations for the school culture. As noted previously, though, adding yet another program is not always the best option—any school can set its own norms, independent of specific programs. The following list provides a few stable ways to norm a culture with positive expectations.

- Adopt a character education program, or revamp and reinvigorate an existing program. Alternatively, come to a consensus with your leadership team on three to five character traits that represent strong values in the school culture. Post them schoolwide and weave them into routine classroom procedures, school events, competitions, and rallies.
- Hold regular monthly awards for a predefined set of high standards such as attendance, grades, growth, citizenship, character, attitude, and so on. Also think about holding an annual award ceremony to begin or close the year celebrating the best of the monthly awards.
- Establish positivity norms for teaching staff, requiring a balance of praise to criticism in classroom instruction. Establish similar norms for teacher-parent communication.
- Host regular lunches, breakfasts, or dinners with high- and low-performing students to establish relationships and incentivize increased or continued effort.
- Plan special academic nights to feature student work and ongoing effort.
- Hold school parties to celebrate the finish of high-stress testing cycles.

Again, the actual programs and efforts implemented will vary from school to school, but the key is to have an intentional focus on positive culture. Once you settle on your frameworks and routines for this process, make these ongoing norms integral components of the school.

Special Population Norms

Special education students and English learners are important to keep in mind in the conversation about norms. Specialized programs should not operate separately from the rest of the school. These students and the staff who work with them are another segment of the school that contributes to the whole. In some schools, these populations may represent a very large percentage of the whole. School norms must be written in a way that can apply equitably across all populations. Consistency in norms will help establish a culture of inclusivity and accessibility in your school. Also be aware, if school norms can't be met by special populations, there are legal implications.

It is a good idea for your administrative team to spend time evaluating existing programs to weigh whether or not they provide equitable access or equitable entry for all students. Consider the following examples lacking equity.

- **Proposed School Health Norm:** "All classes will take thirty-second brain breaks every twenty minutes. During brain breaks, classes will stand and do twenty jumping jacks and then return to their seats."

   This practice may be limiting or shameful to those with physical handicaps.

- **Proposed Schoolwide Math Incentive:** "Every Friday, at the end of the week's math lessons, the two students who can answer the challenge problem fastest receive a star-student certificate to take home."

   This practice implies faster students are better than slower students who also answer correctly. Many IEPs require extra time for processing, and this incentive could violate that requirement.

By looking at these examples, a new leader can understand the value of reviewing all school norms to make sure the procedures in place accommodate the entire school population. Many great ideas and incentives are born out of creativity and excitement, so they are typically well intended. However, it's the job of the school leader to filter the excitement and evaluate the content and the risk. It may take a while for your system of norms to solidify in support of the entire population, but the more you can put together before school starts, the more you'll be ready to make small changes on the fly that have serious impact. In the next section, we discuss codifying specific behavioral expectations and procedures.

Codifying Schoolwide and Classroom Procedures

Codification is an increasingly popular enterprise in the field of organizational leadership. In simple terms, codification in schools is the act of systematizing the complete educational process into a well-defined plan. In doing so, codified schools have a clear, concise direction and plan of attack for how to operate and how to achieve their desired outcomes. Similar to the lifesaving practices mentioned at the start of the chapter, codification involves clear directions, detailed descriptions, and uniform expectations. But, codification is hard work. As in the following story, the process of understanding and codifying your school model can be exhaustive and take years.

> We had a highly successful school in Indianapolis, and we had been asked for years to replicate successful programming in additional schools to offer more opportunities to the families in our area. Year after year, we turned down opportunities for a second school, saying no to investments, grants, and enticing new locations. Folks would always ask why we kept saying no. My response was always the same: "We don't know who we are yet. Until we do, we're not ready." In other words, our culture and our processes were still evolving. We needed that to settle in, and we needed to codify. Then we'd be ready to talk replication. It took us six years to stabilize the school and another year to codify it as we organized and systematized every procedure and description involved in our operation. So, it may have taken seven years to feel ready for expansion, but now we have a codified manual on how to run our entire operation, from academics to facilities. It still takes an amazing team to run the ship, but we're focused, and better suited for doing this whole crazy thing now that we truly know who we are.

Codifying your model involves taking into account everything involved in its operation so you can optimize systems and have them run the way you want. A codified model is one that runs smoothly and consistently because the processes and procedures have been established, improved on, and documented. A well-codified system can be run accurately by multiple people because it has been documented.

For a new leader or a veteran leader in an evolving setting, codification is typically out of reach in the first few years. Everything is still new and shifting in response to daily challenges. In these new settings, the best approach is to keep track of and write down every new rule and process as each one is implemented. This is somewhat labor intensive, but once your new system begins to stabilize, these draft rules for operation will be your initial lists for system codification.

After those initial lists are established, they should grow with each new successfully implemented practice. Share them regularly with staff so there is a common understanding and adapt them dynamically as the school grows. Commitment to this process will put you in a place to create your own robust codification document. If pulling all of that information together into a cohesive document is daunting, hiring an outside consultant to help you organize the many different systems and lists will speed up the completion of the project. In the end, your process of norming systems and organizing them into a plan will give your program the efficiency boost it needs to get on its feet and thrive.

Remember, the codification process will take time. You have to start small. Initially, you can set your school up for starting the process by establishing a simple, focused set of schoolwide and classroom-level procedures and routines. It is critical to teach students exactly what you expect of them, both in the classroom and as they make their way around the building. Beginning the moment they enter the building in the morning and continuing with how they behave during instruction, students are much more likely to meet expectations if they are explicitly told how they are supposed to navigate the school day. One of the biggest mistakes you can make as a leader is *assuming* students will know how to enter the building in an orderly manner, keep their voices at an appropriate level in the hallways, and so on. Likewise, it is a major mistake to assume that all your staff have consistent expectations for students or know how to teach and rehearse the expectations. Students and staff alike benefit from consistent norms clearly outlining such expectations.

As the principal, you need to decide how prescriptive you want to be regarding the classroom-level procedures that teachers must develop. To some extent, this is a matter of personal style, but at a minimum we recommend that you require teachers to have routines for the following classroom procedures.

- Entering the classroom
- Starting warm-up or "do now" activities
- Taking attendance

- Collecting homework
- Getting students' attention
- Moving around the room
- Requesting to leave the room to go to the bathroom, nurse, or office
- Working in small groups
- Asking questions
- Requesting supplies
- Exiting the classroom

Each teacher should have a script for these common classroom-level procedures prior to the first day of school. You may encourage teams of teachers to coauthor the procedures to ensure a common language across grade levels or interdisciplinary teams. Or, you may want to design these procedures with all your staff and require teachers throughout the building to use the same procedures. Whichever approach you prefer, it is crucial to make this clear to your teachers prior to the opening of school. When possible, provide time on teacher report days prior to the start of the school for teachers to write and rehearse their classroom procedures with a peer or someone from the leadership team to ensure a smooth rollout in the first days of the school year.

In addition to defining classroom procedures, we recommend developing clear schoolwide procedures that all students follow and all staff enforce. This will require a coordinated plan for how staff members teach. Rehearse procedures with students in the first days of the school year; the time invested will pay huge dividends as the year progresses. We recommend writing step-by-step procedures and providing time to train students on the following expectations for common areas throughout the school building.

- School entry
- Hallway behavior
- Voice levels
- Cafeteria procedures
- Media center procedures
- Bathroom procedures
- Locker procedures
- Gymnasium and locker room procedures
- School exit

Depending on the amount of time available prior to opening day, some leaders develop these procedures with a committee of staff members representing various grade levels and content teams. If time does not allow for this collaborative approach your first year, that is understandable; however, it is critical for your leadership team to develop these procedures so students will know the expectations from the first moment they enter the building.

There are several resources you can use to develop your school's list of procedures that will become your cultural systems. For example, education author Doug Lemov's 2015 book, *Teach Like a Champion 2.0*, provides an overview of daily routines such as how students line up at the classroom door, how students enter the room and begin class, how students raise their hands appropriately, and so on. For example, Lemov's technique called "Strong Start" defines three phases of a purposeful beginning to classroom instruction: (1) Door to Do Now, (2) Do Now, and (3) Review Now. He then specifically scripts student actions from the moment they enter the classroom (Door to Do Now), to starting a warm-up activity (Do Now), through the teacher going over the warm-up assignment (Review Now). This is one example of a very specific, detailed approach to classroom procedures and training students on expectations. Some schools appreciate this level of specificity while others believe in a less regimented approach.

By now, you likely have an idea of how you'd like many of your school systems to function. Be aware, however, that the complexities inherent in your school will test your structure and can jeopardize the continuity you seek in discipline and behavior. Remember to create systems for positive behavior (for instance, with programs such as PBIS), and to create a balance between positive practices and disciplinary practices. This will help you avoid codifying an oppressive system. That said, it's still important to streamline your discipline and behavior practices. To help with that, the following section describes considerations for responding to student misbehavior.

Responding Appropriately to Misbehavior

Response to misbehavior is one of the most important areas for defining norms and expectations. There are five aspects of discipline systems that leaders should codify regardless of location, school type, or age level.

1. Classroom management
2. Tiers of behavioral support
3. Levels of infractions

4. Process ownership
5. Expulsion and zero-tolerance policies

We detail each one in the following sections to guide you as you adapt your own norms for the same categories.

Classroom Management

The classroom teacher is typically the first level of discipline in any system. Except for less structured times like before school and lunch period, students spend almost the whole day in the classroom, making it the focal point for establishing a culture of discipline. As the school leader, you should work with teachers to make the classroom management system an extension of schoolwide norms. As with a common language, classroom expectations and norms around discipline and behavior should be duplicated class to class and grade to grade. This allows your teachers to speak a common discipline and behavior language. Using similar language throughout the school also reduces problems because no individual class or teacher appears stricter or more lenient.

As part of classroom behavior norms, there are certain ineffective practices that you should ask staff not to use. These include whole-class penalties, shouting, and lectures on behavior—all examples of student shaming (Goodman & Cook, 2019). Your teachers should never employ these tactics. When teachers address a large group with a nonspecific concern or in a hostile manner, there is no direct message to any individual student. Those redirects attempt to create change through guilt and are not likely to provide the desired outcome, so limit the use of whole-class consequences as a schoolwide norm.

Empty threats are also damaging to a normed culture. They can actually train students to misbehave (Darling, 2011). Teachers struggling with misbehavior often get flustered and make exasperated statements like, "One more time and you're in trouble," or, "Knock it off, Jeffrey." In each of those statements, there is no clear directive for change, no direct prompt for how to improve, and no specific consequence. Instead, it communicates that when the teacher threatens, nothing happens. Never allow your staff to make empty threats—if they call out bad behavior, have them apply a nonemotional consequence.

Another great example of this issue is the "count to ten" method. A teacher gives a student until the count of ten to cease a misbehavior. Between one and four, there is usually no behavior change. Between four and seven, the behavior often worsens in an attempt to complete the bad thing the student is doing. Between eight and nine, the behavior improves, and at ten, it usually (hopefully) stops. The student learns not to worry about the first 80 percent of the demand for correction. A better system would be counting to two. At two, you're allowing for some reaction time for behavior to correct, but you're not allowing nine seconds of continued misbehavior. More immediate expectations and consequences, such as receiving behavior marks (on students' behavior tracking charts) or removal from the classroom for a restorative conversation, help prevent empty threats.

Tiers of Behavioral Supports

Creating a tiered system of behavioral supports helps staff identify who is supposed to intervene and when to escalate a response to the next tier. Systems like response to intervention (RTI), multitiered systems of supports (MTSS; Jackson, 2017), and PBIS (Sugai & Horner, 2019) are examples of tiered strategies for proactively serving the behavioral needs of the student population. These processes are outlined in detail in *Taking Action* (Buffum, Mattos, & Malone, 2018) and *An Educator's Guide to Schoolwide Positive Behavioral Interventions and Supports* (Harlacher & Rodriguez, 2017). With the appropriate tiers and structure, "school discipline has the potential to foster safe, respectful, and positive schools, where students learn self-discipline and appropriate problem-solving skills" (Mayworm & Sharkey, 2014, p. 703). Consider the following questions.

- Is it the teacher's job to manage a student's behavior when he or she is prevented from teaching because of a disruption, or is it an administrator's job?
- Who chooses which students get suspended—teachers, the dean, or the principal?
- Do students removed from the classroom get sent to the principal or dean, or do they go to an alternative environment?
- Are alternative environments for students not meeting classroom expectations available on site?
- Are there common forms for all tiers of discipline reports?
- How does the counselor contribute to the discipline process?
- Is there a parent engagement plan woven into the discipline process?

Levels of Infractions

In any system, you'll want to identify levels of infractions. Regardless of what you call the levels, they help teachers and other staff respond appropriately, so gum chewing isn't treated the same as fighting. Every setting needs a definition of what qualifies as a low-level or minor infraction versus a high-level or major infraction. For example, a school might use a three-tier, two-level approach—three tiers of behavioral management, and two levels of infractions. The first tier is the general classroom. The second and third tiers are alternative classrooms with extra academic and behavioral support. Level 1 infractions are handled by the teacher and require a phone call home. Level 2 infractions are handled by the administrative team and also require that team to call home. At the third tier, level 2 infractions are severe and require immediate administrative and parent attention. These situations are case by case and may eliminate a student's return to the regular classroom for the remainder of the day. Similar to this example, making sure your system has a stable set of leveled protocols for discipline infractions will help create consistency.

Prior to the start of the school year, the leadership team should review these levels and protocols for response. Everyone needs to understand what student actions result in which disciplinary reactions. This can be done through repeated practice, by discussing the myriad infractions that can occur within the school and working through the correct responses and outcomes. This process can also be brought to life by working with mock case studies. This is one way to provide an interactive approach to training. By mocking up disciplinary case studies (carefully prepared by the administrative team as an anonymous amalgamation of prior experience), behavioral and educational staff can simulate standard disciplinary situations. By utilizing these scenarios, staff can come together in training to grapple with tough discipline situations and review proper protocol for reaction, communication, and reporting.

Process Ownership

Once you have a discipline process, someone needs to take responsibility for each part of it. We cannot prescribe who should own which piece of the discipline process in your school, but we can emphasize that someone needs to administer each of those parts. There should be a clear delineation of responsibility for every portion of the process. For instance, if your system dictates that the school dean calls home when a student is sent out of a classroom, then that dean must always make the call. Consistency is key for maintaining norms and stable relationships among staff, students, and families.

The point remains that if there are tiers and levels within a discipline system, all involved need to know which part they own. Your system documentation needs to spell it out, and everyone involved should rehearse the process. Staff members who are not involved in a specific procedure should stand back and let it run as intended.

Expulsion and Zero-Tolerance Policies

Expulsion and zero-tolerance policies are difficult and controversial topics. While originally well intended as a response to violent and illegal behavior, zero-tolerance policies are often misapplied and ineffective. They fail to deter first offenses or prevent repeat behaviors (Harlacher, 2015). Similarly, expulsion as a consequence of extreme or repeated misbehavior is often applied inconsistently or in a biased manner. Further, expulsion is detrimental to students' futures, with significant effects on dropout and incarceration rates (American Bar Association, 2016; Coalition for Juvenile Justice, 2019).

That said, there may be rare occasions when suspension or expulsion is necessary. If a student brings a loaded weapon to school, distributes drugs on campus, or assaults a classmate, such a flagrantly illegal act will likely result in a suspension or expulsion, per state law. Zero-tolerance policies become problematic when schools use suspension and expulsion for routine discipline. For instance, a zero-tolerance fighting policy is very tricky—*fighting* is too subjective. Was it play fighting, threats of fighting, or a swing and a miss? Did someone throw something and almost start a fight? An inflexible policy inevitably leads to overapplication. We recommend avoiding zero-tolerance policies as they too often don't account for case-by-case subjectivity. When in doubt about a suspension or expulsion, consult your board, superintendent, and legal counsel for advice.

This is a sensitive and site-specific topic, but if you're in an existing school or school system, there will likely be expulsion policies in place. Get to know them. If you're in a new setting, you may be creating them. If an incident arises in which you may need to enforce such policies, it will be a difficult situation to navigate. Our advice is to document everything, and always consider the safety of your school community. Consult your mentors and other area leaders on these decisions—there are plenty of others in your professional circles who can speak from experience. Lastly, never initiate an expulsion without support from those in positions above you. Many expulsion cases are appealed, so it's important to have your supervisors' support.

These topics we've just discussed are central to norming a discipline and behavior system. You can use the following six questions to customize these elements of the system for your setting.

1. **Classroom management:** What are the schoolwide classroom management expectations?

2. **Tiers of behavioral supports:** What layers of support are available for varying tiers of behavioral issues?

3. **Levels of infractions:** What systems are in place for handling specific behaviors?

4. **Process ownership:** Who has site-specific ownership of discipline and behavioral management, from phone calls to paperwork to consequences?

5. **Expulsion:** What is the philosophy and process for expulsions?

6. **Zero tolerance:** Does your school have a zero-tolerance policy? Is it clearly articulated, or is it case-specific?

*Visit **go.SolutionTree.com/leadership** to download a free reproducible version of these questions.*

>
> **Pause & Reflect**
>
> Can you describe your own behavioral system in simple terms? Are your processes normed and adequate for dealing with the complexities of student behavior?

Keeping Students on Track Academically

The previous section discussed creating a codified system for behavioral management. Here, we focus on the academic side of discipline. In other words, what happens to the student when he or she is removed from the classroom? Your discipline plan is not just about punishment; the discipline process can and should involve the full range of school services, including academics. If a student spends four out of five days out of the classroom due to discipline, that student should still have the opportunity for a quality education. It might not look like the education other students are receiving, but he or she still needs to learn. The ultimate goal is re-entry into the classroom, so neglecting academics while students are removed would put them behind on their assignments and is antithetical to the desired goal.

The school behavioral counselor plays a critical role here. This counselor will often be the person who supervises and helps students as they de-stress. If you have the staffing capacity, academic interventionists, instructional assistants, and administrative support staff should have a plan to provide cultural, emotional, and academic supports for students as they attempt to refocus and eventually re-enter the classroom. Depending on the size of your school, the full-time equivalents you are given, and the number of staff you can afford, these support systems will look different. But the point is the same: supporting students through their behavior struggles and into re-entry is a critical component in your whole-school program.

The only caution for this part of the discipline system is to make sure that these supports do not inadvertently incentivize further misbehavior. You never want the disciplinary consequence and subsequent rehabilitation to be perceived as so interesting or fun that the student will try to get out of the classroom and repeat the process. Because of this, be sure that academic and emotional support work are intentional, rigorous when applicable, appropriately challenging for the student's ability level, and directly in line with classroom expectations.

Summary

In this chapter, we discussed several topics related to schoolwide norms and behavior expectations. It's important to build a foundation of positive, equitable norms so that students know what is expected of them. Codify schoolwide and classroom procedures to ensure consistency. Finally, you need a system for responding to misbehavior that defines tiers of support and levels of infractions, along with clear responsibilities for staff. However, do not neglect the academic needs of students who struggle with appropriate behavior. Next, we take a detailed look at academic systems.

Chapter 5 Reflection Questions

1. How would you describe your school in a way that others would understand? How does that description inform the need to codify your model?

2. Think about your current school structure. How many systems are currently codified into lists or processes? Which systems are priorities to be organized in the near future?

3. Think about the many moving pieces involved in the start of the school day. How much of that start is scripted for staff, students, and parents?

4. Consider the balance of your positive behavior supports and disciplinary systems. Which of those two systems is more structured in your model?

5. How does your school transition a student from a negative disciplinary setting to a positive classroom re-entry?

CHAPTER 6
Develop Academic Systems

Should school leaders allow classroom teachers to determine the academic systems and processes to be utilized in the classroom? We're always surprised at how many diverse answers we get to that simple question. While it's always a great practice to support and empower teachers and gain mutual buy-in for academic decision making, handing over total academic control to the teaching staff can be very problematic. The school leader should always be the academic leader; even if delegated appropriately, the academic responsibility of the school still belongs to the principal. Without solid academic systems, the schoolwide approach can fracture into a class-by-class iteration of how each individual teacher interprets the academic approach. This can lead to an erosion of the academic model and negatively impact student achievement. To avoid this fractured approach, it's important to have a solid grasp on the processes for academic implementation in your school.

Academics and Engagement

As described in chapter 5 (page 85), established norms in school systems reduce repeated errors and tension and increase the efficiency and impact you need to achieve long-term results. However, leaders sometimes overemphasize norms by shortchanging academic time in favor of orientation and rules rehearsals. We've seen examples of schools that use up the first few weeks of school doing nothing more than training students in the school's behavior expectations and culture. This approach is a detriment to academics, which, after all, are still the heart of school. Leaders need to find a balance. We describe several approaches to this concept in the following sections, but first we encourage you to pause and reflect on your own initial experience at school.

> **Pause & Reflect**
>
> Think back to your experiences as a student, a teacher, and an administrator.
> - What did the first few days or weeks of school feel like?
> - Was it all routines and rote exercises to grind in the culture, or was there a faster introduction to academic work?
> - What is your position on rigor at the start of the year?

Chaos Prevention

Once the doors open and the students file in, there is much to do in terms of establishing rules, procedures, schedules, rehearsals, and relationship building. The more chaotic or stressed the population, the more focus teachers are likely to place on these opening rituals. The problem, however, with fixating on norms to start the school year and turning the focus to academics later is that when educators spend all their energy just managing the stress of the moment, they may not have enough energy remaining for managing education and growth. Consider the following comparison to parenting.

> **A Parenting Parable**
>
> Brent and Molly were in their fourth year of marriage with two children: Mallory, age three, and Michael, age one. Since Michael's birth, the household ritual was exciting, but seemed to border on confusion. Molly's exhaustion from incessant evening child care, stacked on top of both her and Brent's daily work schedule, left little room for organizing the home. As soon as the pair felt like they were getting ahead at home, another daily duty or sudden child need would undo the work they'd done. With the constant commotion, it felt like they would never find peace, order, or at least a few consecutive hours of sleep.
>
> During a holiday visit from Molly's mother, Candice, Molly explained how she had reached an exasperated and mentally weary limbo. Confiding in her mother in the absence of the children, she asked the following question:
>
> "Mom, when does it get easier?"
>
> "Easier?" Candice asked.
>
> "Yes," Molly answered. "When does this all settle down?"

"Molly," Candice said with a gentle smile, "it doesn't."

"Then how did you handle it?" Molly asked. "How did you get through it all?"

"Molly," Candice replied, as her smile grew wider, "I did it one day at a time, and I made every day count."

And there it was. Reality had finally soaked in for Molly. She had been crippled by a circular pattern of work that had totally wrecked her sense of order and direction. Even though all the efforts she'd made for household control were under the intention of doing what was best for her children, she had begun to lose hope because she was finding it too hard to cope without finding a solution that would lessen the load. But her mother's words were an instant aha moment. It finally made sense to her that it was always going to be challenging. There was not going to be a magic solution that made the stress and the workload go away, so Molly was able to let go of the notion that one day it was all going to become easy. In that respect, the words from her mother were a gift. For the first time in her three-year run into parenthood, the rules of her game had finally been spelled out. Molly's new understanding was that being in charge of children is hard work, constant work, and worthy work.

Like many new teachers and new school leaders, Molly and Brent had lived as if the challenges of working with and supporting children would eventually soften, and their prior life and comfortable way of living would return. But, once they understood that duty and distraction would rule the household for an indeterminable future, both parents could relax their need for control, and prioritize the most important part of the family: the care of their children, and the molding of their future.

Fast-forward three months later, and Molly's evenings had changed. On returning home from work, the evening routine was already in place. Brent began each night by cooking dinner. While he did that, Molly's job was to have reading time with both children. After dinner, Molly did the dishes as Brent bathed the kids. Then, it was more reading time with Brent and Mallory, while Molly had playtime with Michael, changed him one last time, and put him to bed. Molly would then join Brent and tuck Mallory in, which had become something of a singsong ritual with variations of the ABC song.

With the children in bed, the pair would return to themselves, wading into a living room scattered with clutter, putting everything back in its place—knowing full well it would be a mess again in the morning. When all was tidy, they sat in front of the television, enjoying a show together while catching up on some emails. But, within this newfound routine, the

> element of desperation and despair had all but vanished. This job of taking care of children was now their responsibility, and they had chosen this path. Now that they had accepted it for the challenging task that it was, they developed a detailed plan for investing their energy in their children. If the house was a mess, so be it—at least the kids got a healthy meal, a bath, and some quality time. If they were both exhausted, then they could sleep in the knowledge that they were tired for a good cause. And, if the routine declined, the kids would quickly remind them (by getting out of hand) that it was time to get back to the plan.
>
> While it doesn't mean they lived happily ever after, it illustrates how they found a way to accept the rules of the game they were in, and to leverage systems and engagement to make better sense of their day-to-day struggle.

This is a healthy dose of sappy allegory, but the point is to illustrate the parallel between the family experience of Molly and Brent, and the school experience common to a new school leader or teacher. Parents and educators reading this bit of print will quickly relate, because working with children is an elastic art form. There is no singular manual, training, or college that can properly prepare an adult for appropriately caring for a child, let alone hundreds of children. But, if all energy is exhausted just to pull order from an endless list of tasks, there isn't enough energy remaining for education and growth. So, there must be some method to the madness of growth amidst the barrage of work.

There is tried-and-true science (Horng, Klasik, & Loeb, 2010) related to this problem at the school level that illustrates the important need to prioritize work in areas that can influence positive change (such as focusing more on organizational management rather than day-to-day instruction). This concept correlates well to the field of parenting (Brieant, Holmes, Deater-Deckard, King-Casas, & Kim-Spoon, 2017), again demonstrating that the inconsistencies of chaotic home decision making can negatively impact child development. Knowing what works and what doesn't can simplify the task of chaos prevention. The suggestions of the research all boil down to proper prioritization, delegation, and winnable battles. We can reduce chaos when we focus on the appropriate tasks, and within those, we prioritize the things we can control. You see, for the principal, teacher, or parent, the act of controlling chaos is often counterintuitive. We all want to react to chaos, but the appropriate solution is proactive. Classroom chaos should be handled with high engagement instead of reactive knee-jerk decision making.

Teachers need to establish rules, order, and relationships, but if the focus of a school is on maintaining order, then the result will be a staff that spends all their time on rules, order, and relationships. That task on its own can be a full-time job and may not create a pathway for student academic growth. To create a calm, structured environment that is also successful academically, the focus on student learning should start immediately with engagement. Rules and relationships are part of the system, but high academic engagement is the key to keeping chaos in check. Once engagement becomes the daily goal, the routines become effective. Think back to the story of Molly and Brent. They created a sequence of engagement for their children, and the engagement created order and reduced stress. When engagement fell off, the stress increased and reminded them to get back on schedule. Classroom academic engagement is very similar. A highly engaged lesson with extensions and multiple opportunities for work when finished is a behavioral management tool as much as it is an academic tool.

Long story short, don't fall into the trap of spending the first few weeks of school establishing rules and norms with the idea of settling into an academic routine when the time is right, or the classes are ready. Have the routine prepared and ready, with an invigorating dose of engagement built in. If things aren't working, then re-evaluate where the system is loose and increase the engagement.

Active Engagement Versus Compliance

So you're ready to start with high engagement on day one, but the next concern is sustaining ample engagement once students become habituated to routines. Once your students accept the rigor of the daily routine, chaos is sure to diminish. Another productivity problem may then begin to surface: are your students engaged or just compliant? Students sitting in rows of desks, quietly writing while the teacher monitors from the front of the room, signify a very orderly, composed classroom. But are these students mentally tuned in and learning? Who's to say they aren't strategizing their next social media posts, thinking about the game after school, or daydreaming about the latest drama in their friend groups? Students need to be actively working and learning, not just behaving. Their developing brains depend on it. Consider the following story.

> **Ms. Johnson's Mathematics Class**
>
> In Susie Johnson's seventh-grade mathematics class, on any given day you can witness a consistent routine of high student engagement that's eminently compatible with the needs of the adolescent brain. As students

enter the room and begin their do-now exercise, she reviews the agenda and learning objectives so students understand what they need to know and be able to do. She always provides a do-now exercise and a minilesson with teacher modeling at the beginning of the period, followed by cooperative learning time with at least three different extensions that students move into if they finish the initial assignment early. Examples of her extensions include math manipulatives, cooperative challenges, small-group or one-on-one remediation tasks (strategically assigned by Ms. Johnson for reviewing problems missed on homework or a recent test), practice problems based on the minilesson, or spiral review of critical skills.

As Ms. Johnson works through the lesson, she refers to the learning objectives often and uses them in a strong closure activity and mini-assessment at the end. She always returns to the learning objectives at the end of class and asks students to demonstrate their level of mastery on the objectives via an exit ticket or other quick check for understanding. In Ms. Johnson's room, students' minds are continually activated and processing information in a variety of ways to meet all students' learning styles, and she has proof of their learning at the conclusion of the lesson.

Ms. Johnson has obviously taken rote compliance out of her lesson design. Her engagement cycle is structured with standards-driven delivery, observation, feedback, extension, and frequent checks for understanding. This style of implementation is challenging, especially for inexperienced teachers. As a leader developing academic systems and managing a variety of teachers, consider providing a checklist of engagement methods and activities as a tool for annual trainings, feedback on norms, and weekly classroom walkthroughs for making sure classroom processes move beyond simple compliance. Although engaging lesson design can take on many forms depending on the grade level and content area, the sample checklist in figure 6.1 shows how teachers might go beyond simple compliance.

Engagement is essential for learning *and* for classroom management; as such, it should form the foundation of instruction. Unfortunately, the teacher's style of instruction and the students' level of engagement tend to vary widely from classroom to classroom. We address this problem in the next section.

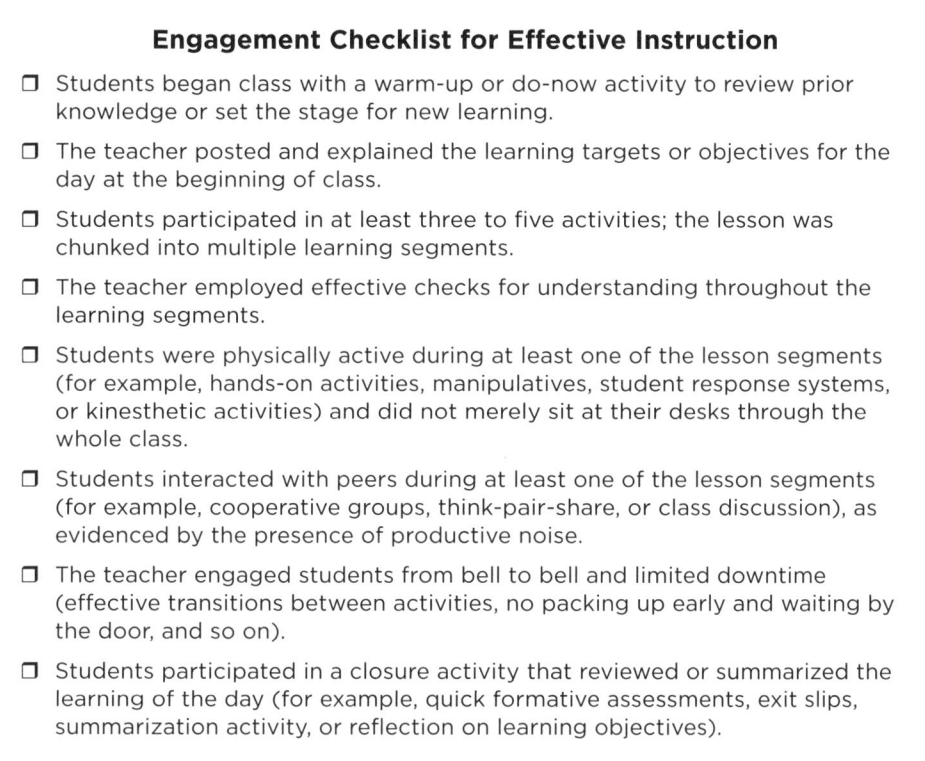

Figure 6.1: Sample checklist of engagement strategies.

Visit ***go.SolutionTree.com/leadership*** *to download a free reproducible version of this figure.*

The Case for Codification and Simplification

In chapter 2, we mentioned that there is both an art and a science to education, not only in the classroom but also in leadership. Teachers are individuals with strengths, weaknesses, and the ability to personalize their instruction and respond on the fly, exemplifying the art of education. On the science side, however, there are research-based strategies that every educator can use to teach more effectively.

In this section, we focus on the science. A manageable set of proven strategies goes a long way toward consistently high-quality education throughout a school. As we mentioned at the start of this chapter, in the absence of any guidance in this area, teachers will run their classrooms as they see fit—some will be great, but others will flounder. On the other end of the spectrum, schools may also impose a laundry list of initiatives and programs that are too numerous and disconnected for teachers to use effectively. This causes confusion among staff; teachers are unsure how to successfully implement everything on the list, so they end up picking and choosing, or only partially executing. Both of these cases lead to great variances between classrooms, and great variances in curriculum and instruction throughout a school lead to variances in educational quality and student learning outcomes. In other words, a school becomes an educational lottery.

Understanding the Problem of Variance

To better understand the problem of instructional variance, reflect on the following case studies.

Coach Compton

Mr. Compton is a sixth-grade mathematics teacher who has been teaching for four years. He enjoys his students and likes teaching, but more importantly, he loves coaching football. If he could coach full-time, he would do so. He doesn't have much time for or interest in lesson planning, so on Monday morning of a typical week, he can be found stopping into fellow math teacher Ms. Griffin's classroom to ask what they're supposed to be teaching that week. On this particular Monday morning, Ms. Griffin tells him that ratio tables are next in the curriculum, and he replies, "Oh, that's right. Thanks." Mr. Compton proceeds back to his classroom to find the chapter in the textbook on ratio tables. As students arrive, he welcomes them and then goes to the board to demonstrate a few practice problems on ratio tables, reading and working through problems straight from the textbook. Students sit quietly and watch Mr. Compton solve ratio tables on the board. After he completes the first four problems, he tells the class to complete problems 5–20 on page 110 on their own. Students work silently and independently. With five minutes remaining in the period, he tells the students that if they are not finished, they should complete the rest of the problems for homework. Most students close their books and line up at the door to wait for the bell.

Ms. Griffin

Ms. Griffin is a sixth-grade mathematics teacher who has been teaching for four years. She teaches next door to Mr. Compton. She loves her students and loves teaching. With a few years of experience, she now feels she's hitting her stride. She fully understands her administration's expectations for curriculum and instruction and is able to customize them for her own teaching style and personality to align the school's expectations with her own. As her students arrive in class on this particular Monday morning, they are greeted by a warm-up assignment on the board that includes four review problems to activate their learning from the prior lesson. She sets a timer for five minutes and then circulates around the room returning students' graded exit tickets from the prior lesson. She stops briefly at a few students' desks to explain in more detail the written feedback she provided on the exit ticket problems they missed. When the timer sounds, Ms. Griffin reviews the warm-up problems with the class and then presents the learning objectives for today's lesson. She then moves into direct instruction by modeling how to complete a ratio table, building on the students' previously learned skills. She stops periodically for turn-and-talks and checks for understanding to ensure students are truly engaged in the new content and learning through her modeling. When she feels students are confident in this new information, she releases them to small-group practice followed by independent practice. With five minutes remaining in the period, Ms. Griffin distributes exit tickets with two questions on ratio tables so that they can demonstrate their learning and show whether they are on track to achieve the lesson's learning goal. When the bell rings, students pack up and drop their completed exit tickets in the labeled container by the door as they exit the classroom.

This teaching dichotomy plays out in far too many districts across the country. Two teachers coexist in a school or even right next door to each other, yet students continue to receive such different learning experiences. It's clear that the students' learning will vary greatly depending on which teacher they happen to be assigned to. These case studies reflect the all-too-common educational lottery that students are subjected to in school. The luck of the draw in the master schedule determines if a student will be assigned a quality teacher who will meet his or her needs and engender growth that school year. Likewise, a roll of the scheduling dice will sentence hundreds of students to a year of diminished, if any, academic growth at the hands of ineffective teachers.

Pause & Reflect

As a leader aspiring to make an impact on your school, what will you do to decrease this kind of variance? If you inherited a school with a dichotomy like that of Mr. Compton and Ms. Griffin, how would you respond to the issue?

What compounds this problem is the fact that our weakest teachers are often relegated to teaching the neediest students. These are typically teachers of students from ethnic minority and low socioeconomic backgrounds. For these subsets of students, teacher quality can be the fulcrum of success or failure. Heather G. Peske and Kati Haycock (2006), authors of *Teaching Inequality: How Poor and Minority Students Are Shortchanged on Teacher Quality*, describe the problem this way: "Students who have three highly effective teachers in a row score more than 50 percentile points above their counterparts who have three ineffective teachers in a row—even when they started with the same score" (p. 11). The negative impacts of an ineffective teacher are often irreversible; therefore, developing highly effective teachers is a primary obligation of a principal. Eliminating the educational lottery in schools is a moral imperative.

Of course, the simplest solution would be to fire inadequate teachers or decline to renew their contracts for the next year. However, in addition to the staffing shortages this would cause, some districts, states, or provinces make evaluating out poorly performing teachers or placing them on performance improvement plans a lengthy, laborious process. Local policies or contracts may require up to a full school year of observations, paperwork, and meetings with the teacher and perhaps with union representatives to build an ample case for nonrenewal. In cases where a school's principal doesn't build a sufficient case for a teacher's nonrenewal, the district leadership will sometimes transfer the ineffective teacher to another building for a different principal to begin the process all over again. In these cases, it's the students who truly suffer. Consider the following case study.

An Unexpected Hire

An elementary school principal receives an unexpected visit from the district's human resources director. The conversation proceeds like this:

"Principal Hughes, as the school year is wrapping up, we have been informed that one of the other elementary principals is not planning to renew the contract of one of his assistant principals, Mr. Grant. The principal has been disappointed in Mr. Grant's performance for some time now. However, he did not appropriately document Mr. Grant's deficiencies, nor did he develop an improvement plan for him, so while we have decided not to renew Mr. Grant's administrative contract, we are offering him a teaching position somewhere in the district. He has an elementary teaching license, and . . . you see, Mrs. Hughes, your school is the only elementary school that currently has an opening. So, Mr. Grant will be assigned to teach third grade in your building in the upcoming school year."

> "Wow," Mrs. Hughes replied. "I have been interviewing some outstanding candidates for that opening, as you instructed me to do. As a matter of fact, I was just about to offer the position to Michelle Rose. You remember her—she's an outstanding teacher with experience who filled in for a maternity leave for us earlier this year. Are you saying I can't bring her on to my team?"
>
> "Unfortunately, that's correct, Mrs. Hughes," the human resources director responded. "The superintendent and school board are concerned that proper protocol was not followed throughout the year, such as informing Mr. Grant prior to winter break that his job might be in jeopardy. So, unfortunately, you have no option but to place Mr. Grant in your vacant third-grade position. I'm so sorry for this inconvenience."

Believe it or not, this situation is not uncommon in the world of school administration. Mrs. Hughes had no control over the addition of Mr. Grant to her staff. Even if she does her due diligence and follows the performance evaluation protocol leading to nonrenewal of his contract at the end of the next school year, an entire class of students will experience a full year of inadequate teaching and varying degrees of learning loss at a key developmental age. Their parents may rightfully raise concerns about the obvious lack of rigor, adding even more stress to Mrs. Hughes's efforts to document the issue. In this case study, Principal Hughes was doing all the right things, but was faced with a situation that was out of her hands. While these disappointing situations do occur, there are still many ways to control the things you are able to control, reduce variance, and improve teacher quality in your school.

Creating Consistency

Teachers won't succeed in an environment where success is dependent on too many variables. Accounting for this is the key to creating consistency. In *Good to Great and the Social Sectors*, business management expert Jim Collins (2005) makes this case:

> The real path to greatness, it turns out, requires simplicity and diligence. It requires clarity, not instant illumination. It demands each of us to focus on what is vital—and to eliminate all of the extraneous distractions. . . . We need to define our priorities with piercing clarity and say "no, thank you" to anything that would divert us from successfully implementing them. (p. 17)

Leadership expert Marcus Buckingham (2005) also writes about clarity, defining it as "the antidote to anxiety" and emphasizing "if you do nothing else as a leader, be clear" (p. 146). Educational researcher Mike Schmoker (2011) pushes this point a step further:

> Leaders must be seen as clarifiers, focusers, "keepers of the core" who incessantly cut through the clutter to distinguish between what is merely important and what is imperative. . . . It's this simple: If we want better schools, we have to monitor the implementation of our highest priorities. (p. 18)

High-performing schools such as Adlai E. Stevenson High School in Lincolnshire, Illinois, have proven the effectiveness of the aforementioned theories. Stevenson High School began a journey of improvement in 1983 by first focusing on only two core practices.

1. Directing teams of teachers to create and implement a quality, common curriculum for every course
2. Directing teams of teachers to ensure sound instruction and lessons

Principal Richard DuFour and his team maintained their focus on these priorities for five years before implementing anything else. At a school like Stevenson, there is no educational lottery. There is minimal opportunity for variances in curriculum or core instructional practices between classrooms because the leadership requires that teachers teach the agreed-on essential standards and skills for their courses and implement high-yield instructional strategies and lesson design. For example, all students enrolled in algebra 1 have access to the same guaranteed and viable curriculum whether they have Mr. Jones or Mrs. Smith or Mr. Walker as their teacher. Additionally, students experience similar instructional practices and core lesson design in each classroom. The result is high levels of learning for all students (Schmoker & Schmoker, 2001).

Recall the descriptions of Mr. Compton's and Ms. Griffin's classrooms from the beginning of this chapter (page 108): two teachers with the same number of years of experience in the same building with wildly different levels of performance. What is the role of school leadership in creating this variance and allowing it to continue? In Mr. Compton's defense, we must ask if an administrator has ever provided a codified framework for teaching and learning and held him accountable to it. Is it possible that his principal is not fulfilling the duties of instructional leadership by codifying the curricular and instructional practices that yield high levels of learning?

In order to decrease the variance between classrooms and to avoid the educational lottery, you must be piercingly clear about your expectations. At a minimum, it's critical to codify the basics of teaching and learning: curriculum, instruction, and assessment.

Don't assume that teachers already know what they should be teaching or how to teach it in the most effective ways. You also can't assume they know how to individualize instruction to meet students' needs or provide ongoing assessments to monitor their students' performance. Your school's curriculum, instruction, and assessment model must be the guide for this and should be established immediately. In this chapter, we provide you with information and ideas to help you lay the groundwork for this model.

As you open your new school or inherit an existing one, think about what you'll do to help teachers succeed. Define your priorities for teaching and learning in a manageable way—give your teachers three to five priority tasks and the tools to enact those tasks successfully. It's important early on to focus on the basics and make these priorities crystal clear to your teaching staff. Even a brand-new teacher should be able to meet expectations given the clear guidelines and resources you provide. Once the priorities are established, create an efficient and focused monitoring system to inspect what you expect. This system can be a simple walkthrough document for you and your administrative team to check on progress. It can also be a weekly feedback form that teachers provide based on their perceived progress toward their priority tasks. Either way, the key is to have a simple tool that doesn't overwhelm, but rather focuses the approach on improvement in the classroom.

To be sure, standardizing expectations and decreasing the variance between classrooms does not mean creating robotic teachers who mechanically follow a rote program. Within curricular and instructional frameworks, there is ample room for individual teachers to be creative in approach and delivery. The codification process simply illuminates boundaries within which teachers should operate and gives them tools for teaching effectively. The quality of curriculum and instruction should be standardized and of a consistently high caliber throughout the school, while also tailored to the unique needs of the students in each classroom. You can think of this like an international franchise restaurant: McDonald's offers the exact same classic cheeseburger and french fries on its menus all around the world, but it also offers additional menu items that align to local cultures. For example, McDonald's menu in China includes several fish options that might not be desired by Chicago patrons. But the core of the menu never changes.

In the following sections, we explore curriculum, instruction, and assessment in greater detail.

What to Teach: A Guaranteed and Viable Curriculum

When it comes to defining what to teach, we recommend a *guaranteed and viable curriculum*. In line with our emphasis on consistency, *guaranteed* means that students in the same grade or course learn the same content regardless of the teacher who instructs them. *Viable* means that there is enough time available to sufficiently address all the content (Marzano, Warrick, & Simms, 2014). Both elements are essential and, taken together, require a schoolwide effort to define a reasonable amount of content for every grade level and course.

A guaranteed and viable curriculum for all students begins with analyzing the state, provincial, or national academic standards your students are expected to learn. This analysis is necessary due to the sheer amount of academic content in most standards documents. Teachers are expected to cover a mind-boggling number of standards in a grade level or course—it's common for there to be seventy to ninety standards assigned to a given content area at a certain grade level. How can teachers possibly teach and assess all of them thoroughly? The reality is, they can't—nor should they. However, the fact remains that the curriculum in every sixth-grade mathematics class in your building, for example, must be identical (that is, guaranteed), which means that you cannot leave curriculum decisions up to individual teachers.

Once again, prioritizing and clarifying are the solutions. The overwhelming list of academic standards needs to be sorted to identify those that are essential and those that are useful but less critical. Education consultant and standards expert Larry Ainsworth (2003, 2013) refers to these categories as *priority standards* and *supporting standards*. Ainsworth (2013) provides a useful definition of these standards. He explains that priority standards are

> a carefully selected *subset* of the total list of the grade-specific and course-specific standards within each content area that students must know and be able to do by the end of each school year in order to be prepared for the standards at the next grade level or course. Priority Standards represent the *assured student competencies* that each teacher needs to help every student learn, and demonstrate proficiency in, prior to leaving the current grade or course. (p. xv)

By contrast, supporting standards are

> those standards that support, connect to, or enhance the Priority Standards. They are taught within the context of the Priority Standards, but do not receive the same degree of instruction and assessment emphasis as do the Priority Standards. The supporting standards often become the *instructional scaffolds* to help students understand and attain the more rigorous and comprehensive Priority Standards. (p. xv)

Teachers are responsible for ensuring that students learn all of the standards; however, not all of them need to be given equal focus. It's your job as a leader to remove the guesswork regarding which standards receive priority. Even better, it's your job as a leader to facilitate a process for your teachers to collaboratively prioritize the standards and map them both horizontally (across each grade level) and vertically (aligned to the next and prior grades). Grade-level or content-area teams of teachers discuss and determine which academic standards are priority standards and which are supporting standards for their courses. To guide decisions, teachers can use the selection criteria in table 6.1.

Table 6.1: Criteria for Priority Standards

Criterion	Definition	Guiding Question	Example
Endurance	This standard will be needed beyond a single grade or course; it will be useful in later life.	Will proficiency on this standard provide students with knowledge and skills that will be valuable beyond the present?	Proficiency in reading and summarizing informational texts will endure throughout a student's academic career and work life.
Leverage	This standard has crossover application within the content area and to other content areas.	Will proficiency on this standard help students make interdisciplinary connections?	Proficiency in creating and interpreting graphs, diagrams, and charts will help students in math, science, social studies, language arts, and other areas.
Readiness	This standard is a prerequisite to enter a new grade level or course of study.	Is proficiency on this standard required for success in the next grade level or course?	Developing an understanding of phonemic awareness must occur before students can read fluently.
External Exams	This is a standard that students will likely encounter on annual standardized tests, college entrance exams, and occupational competency exams.	Which of these standards is the most comprehensive or rigorous?	Citing textual evidence to support analysis of a text is commonly required on standardized tests and other exams.

Source: Adapted from Ainsworth, 2013.

The outcome of this process will be a curriculum that prioritizes the academic standards that teachers will teach in each grade level and content area. It also serves as a codified pacing guide for teachers to navigate the standards in an efficient manner throughout the year. Once you've determined what teachers need to teach, you can easily align your school's curricular materials to the corresponding standards at the appropriate times in the school year and then move into the *how*—instructional practices.

How to Teach It: Instructional Practices

Equally important to defining what teachers should teach is clarifying how they teach it. We are professionals with licenses to practice our craft. As professionals, we have the responsibility to work with the latest and best research in our field. Clearly define your instructional expectations to decrease the variance between classrooms and ensure that all students have access to sound lessons.

There are several research-proven approaches to designing sound lessons that move students toward mastery of academic standards. Whichever lesson planning method you prefer, we encourage you to choose one that is most appropriate for the grade levels of students in your school and pushes students to engage with content standards in a manner that moves them toward mastery of the lesson objectives and standards. In designing lessons, there are a few common rules that can be applied to a wide variety of educational settings. They are as follows.

- Work closely with the state or provincial authority to identify which academic standards are prioritized in each content area at your school's grade levels. Be sure to check if your state or province provides exemplar lessons or topics for high-priority standards.
- Develop weekly lesson plans that reference the academic standards being taught for each specific grade level and subject area.
- Allow the weekly format to break down into daily delivery methods, including references to chapters, worksheets, web resources, and so on.
- Require the submission of all lesson plans to administration. While this sounds tedious, it allows a school to create a bank and record of the yearly plan for each grade level and subject area. It also allows for exemplar lesson plans to be catalogued for use in future years.
- Connect all lesson plans to a yearlong curriculum map. This map should align with state or provincial academic outcomes for the grade level and subject area being taught. Reference mapped connections to the yearlong plan in the weekly lessons.

- Consider utilizing a shared approach or common planning time for grade-level teachers to collaborate on their lesson planning. This can ease the burden of having each teacher design every lesson and can build stronger grade-level, class-to-class instructional consistency.

How to Monitor It: Assessment Practices

In addition to *what to teach* and *how to teach it*, your school's instructional model should include guidelines for assessment practices. Lack of an effective and efficient monitoring system undermines successful deployment of even the most carefully considered instructional practices—teachers can provide excellent instruction on a guaranteed and viable curriculum, but without assessment, the system will fail. Teachers must monitor student learning and performance using a cycle of formative assessment in which students have numerous opportunities to demonstrate their status and growth with respect to a learning target. These assessments provide feedback to students and allow teachers to prescribe interventions and help students continue to progress. Teachers can also examine each student's pattern of formative scores to assign summative ratings, such as those that appear on report cards (Marzano, Norford, & Ruyle, 2019). Students thrive in an environment of high expectations and high support—namely, a setting in which teachers clarify expectations, monitor progress, and provide feedback for improvement or enrichment.

There are several tools that can be used to effectively implement a monitoring system, so we recommend developing the best process that works for you and your school community. Depending on your school community, your district or network may prescribe an assessment system to you, but it is important that you monitor your student population at various intervals so you can gauge growth. Benchmarked assessments that allow for multiple tests throughout the academic year help a school evaluate academic progress and make midyear adjustments on an individual-student and whole-class basis. The ability to make these adjustments is directly tied to sound, nationally normed assessment tools, and is critical to the success of your educational system.

Customization for Students and Communities

Your core instructional program should emphasize *student learning* rather than teaching. As such, it must take your school population and individual students into account. Students acquire skills and knowledge at different paces. Anthony Muhammad (2009), well known for his work on transforming school culture and leadership, describes this concept using an easy-to-understand formula, which illustrates the traditional way we approach teaching in our schools.

$$I(C) + T(C) = L(V)$$
Instruction (constant) *plus* Time (constant) *equals* Learning (varied)

Traditionally, this is the way schools are designed. Students stay in a grade level or course for one school year or one semester, and all receive the same instruction and the same assessments at the same designated times. After each assessment, a score goes in the grade book, and the teacher moves on and repeats the cycle again. As illustrated in the formula, if the instruction is the same for all students and the amount of time available is the same for all students, then the learning will always be the variable. As Muhammad (2009) says, "This formula *guarantees* we will *always* have an achievement gap."

No educators intend to create achievement gaps, but if we don't create a system that can vary the amount of time and instructional support that students receive, then we will continue to create and sustain gaps in student achievement. Now, consider what happens when we switch the variables and constants.

$$I(V) + T(V) = L(C)$$
Instruction (varied) *plus* Time (varied) *equals* Learning (constant)

This change is necessary. As you frame your academic systems, ask yourself, "What do my teachers do to provide varied instruction and time so that learning can be the constant in our school?" We understand that is quite a heavy question, but it is an essential one.

As teachers provide flexible instruction to accommodate individual students, you can consider accommodations for your student population as a whole. Principals cannot implement the same academic systems in every school; leaders need to customize the model based on local circumstances. Each new school setting you work in will have similarities to and differences from your previous experiences. As principals, our job is to create systems that can embrace these differences and generate better outcomes for students and families by developing an academic model that best serves them. In the following sections, we discuss demographic differences, homework versus classwork, blended learning, and guided practice.

Demographic Differences

Wherever your school is located, you'll need to understand your student and parent demographics. Diversity in family support, family background, and student preparedness will dramatically impact your ability to implement an impactful academic model. Every school population is nuanced, with differences in stress, trauma, pride, insecurity, independence, and so on. Your ability to create forward momentum in your system is largely dependent on how you recognize your demographic differences and then respond appropriately to support positive gain. Consider the population interaction chart in figure 6.2 (page 120), which is designed to give principals an idea of how students and families might interact with schools, depending on demographic trends.

> **Pause & Reflect**
>
> Complete the population interaction chart for your school. What is the demographic makeup of the community you serve? How equipped are you and your staff for dealing with the needs and sensitivities that your population presents?

While figure 6.2 is designed as a guide and not a measurable psychological profile, it helps to sharpen a leader's focus on how the population and demographic trends at a school can demand varying levels of attention. Consider the following two case studies.

Cindy Wheeler

Cindy Wheeler was a principal in urban Charlottesville, Virginia. During the first six months of her tenure at a K–5 elementary school, she instituted a mandatory homework policy, dead set on her vision for high school and college preparedness for her third- through fifth-grade students. By February of her first year, 40 percent of her fifth graders and 50 percent of her third graders had failing grades. After numerous parent complaints about the rigidity in the grading system, Cindy met with her upper elementary teaching staff and found out that a surprising 76 percent of the failing students were failing because of late or missing homework.

Later in the school year, those same students took the state exam. Their scores on the state test far exceeded their classroom grades, many by more than 30 percent. Parents were outraged, and Cindy spent her first summer in the hot seat, indignantly scrapping her firm stance on homework to appease her administration.

Directions: Circle the definition that best describes your school's population from the three categories that follow. Then, add the numbers from each circled box. Total the scores and reference the interaction expectations key below the chart.

	1	2	3	4
Socioeconomic Status (SES)	Very Low SES	Low SES	Medium SES	High SES
Enrollment Mobility (MOB)	Homeless	High MOB	Medium MOB	Low MOB
Family Structure and Stability (FSS)	Very Low FSS — Homeless or in foster care with little to no support	Low FSS — Very limited meaningful supports	Medium FSS — Family support is evident, but inconsistent	High FSS — Stable, consistent environment

Total from above: → 0–3 → 4–7 → 8–10 → 11–12

Family Interactions With School	Excitement with skepticism, but trust not developed. Minimal or transactional communication.	Optimistic, some trust established. Reactive communication.	Easygoing due to trust established. Better with frequent touch points.	Great when things go well. Can be either hands off or high touch. Expects detailed, consistent communication.
Student Interactions at School	Lower emotional attachment, projection, behavior swings, needs hands-on learning, high engagement	Stress in social settings, low autonomy, trouble with trust, improves with structure	Rule dependent but becoming autonomous, driven by public praise	Demanding and entitled, but high-functioning, self-motivated, and autonomous

Figure 6.2: Population interaction chart.

*Visit **go.SolutionTree.com/leadership** for a free reproducible version of this figure.*

Dianne and Mr. Naismith

Dianne was a single parent of an eighth-grade student in Miami. Having recently returned from prison, she'd taken custody of her daughter from the family grandmother. Her colorful language and quick outbursts during interactions with the school had the office staff on constant high alert. Her daughter, Becca, was constantly in trouble for repeatedly challenging her teacher during class. Backed by the example of her mom's bullying of the school staff, her defiance was escalating.

The school principal, Mr. Naismith, was a firm disciplinarian with no patience for incessant rule breaking. But Dianne was unrelentingly combative, escalating the tension each time she received a phone call from him about her daughter. By the second month of school, Dianne had reached a breaking point. The constant accusations against her daughter made her feel the school was judging her as a mother. In the school office, she blew up in an expletive-laced tirade, blaming the school for singling out her daughter. She sat herself on the office desk in defiance, refusing to listen to Mr. Naismith, refusing to leave until her daughter's teacher was held accountable, and threatening to call the local news.

Twenty minutes later, Dianne was escorted out of the building in handcuffs, but the damage had been done. As word spread about angry episodes like this one, multiple families and a handful of high-quality teachers left after the first semester. The traumatic culture sparking ongoing conflict between the school and its parents was simply too much for those with access to better options.

In the first example, Cindy failed to take into account her community's capacity for home-based support. Her parent community was unable to accommodate this school policy. This misstep cost Cindy an enormous amount of trust and put her in a difficult position with her board as well.

In the second example, Mr. Naismith was trying to enforce a strong culture of discipline because Becca was clearly violating school rules, but he didn't understand how to best work with Dianne. Had he involved Dianne in the discipline of her daughter in a way that empowered rather than alienated her, maybe there would have been a better outcome. Instead, he accused and belittled an already struggling parent. With her authority in the situation stripped away, Dianne felt she had to react. Her reaction was undeniably extreme, but Mr. Naismith's system had backed Dianne into a corner.

As these case studies imply, there is no scripted solution to every school-parent challenge. Our intention is to illustrate the need for understanding your school community, especially your parents. Whether your community is struggling or highly privileged, every encounter should be handled with sensitivity to the population you serve.

Homework or Classwork

Let's revisit Cindy Wheeler, the principal with high homework expectations. Cindy knew the research—she'd read that homework overload was the exception and that most U.S. students spend no more than sixty minutes each day on homework, regardless of their grade level in school (Loveless, 2014). In addition, the National Parent Teacher Association (National PTA, 2016) recommends that each grade level should receive meaningful, grade-appropriate homework. Cindy was simply heeding expert advice, with the intent of preparing her students for high school and college. So why, if Cindy had followed best practices, had she hit such a brick wall?

Simply put, Cindy had overestimated her parent community's capacity to support schoolwork at home. When a school assigns homework, it inherently assumes a certain level of support from families. Despite high ideals, Cindy had allowed a national best practice to guide her local decision making without assessing whether it could work in her students' homes. In middle- to upper-socioeconomic status (SES) populations, parent support is usually more consistent. In upper-SES communities, it's not uncommon for parents to complain that there isn't enough homework. Clearly, in these settings, homework is accepted as part of the process. In lower-SES settings, households are sometimes less consistent, and can be less capable of support (Bowd, Bowles, & McKenzie, 2016; Núñez et al., 2015). Grading a student on his or her family's inability to support additional work at home is, at the very least, insensitive. Research and best practices are great guides, but the educational approach has to be individualized.

While practice is important for learning, the amount and importance of homework must be aligned with the individual school community. Even in regimented school districts with homework mandates, building leaders have a good amount of local control over this issue. Don't fall into the trap of homogenizing homework without understanding its implications on the parent community. Now let's get back to Cindy Wheeler again. What can she do differently?

> **Cindy Wheeler's New Approach**
>
> Cindy spent her summer trying to reconfigure her research-based approach to homework. Her home-based requirements had been shot down, but

> her belief in the importance of extra student practice remained. So, she moved forward and developed a new policy. Her students would get the same amount of practice as before, only now they'd get that practice in the classroom. She mandated a reduction of teacher-led instructional time, and an increase in student work time. She developed implementation charts with timed expectations and detailed lesson plans with a gradual-release model. Her students would get extended classroom time practicing concepts, and they'd be guided through that practice by their teacher.
>
> At first Cindy's new approach was a wreck, because the new implementation model was a huge departure from the prior year. As teachers adjusted and the approach caught on, though, her classrooms settled down, and student data showed encouraging growth. Fast-forward five years, and Cindy's school became the top in her region. Her school has matured considerably. It now assigns homework per national guidelines, but lowers the weighting on the homework grade so it won't crater student scores. The school carefully tracks alignment of classroom grades to standardized benchmark data. The day-to-day emphasis of the school is on student work in the classroom, with teachers guiding student practice. It was an intense model to implement, but in this form, it became nearly impossible to distinguish between homework and classwork. The two concepts had merged. It wasn't Cindy's original plan, but it became her localized solution.

Cindy's case is one to consider. No matter what demographic variances a new leader may face, students still need time to practice in order to master standards. While a new leader may make an error or two along the way, having the resiliency to put students in the right environment for success is the most important part of the job. In other words, finding the right balance between classwork and homework must be prioritized.

Blended Learning

Technology is increasingly integral to education. Educational technology and blended learning are not just threatening fads; they're already standard expectations of best teaching and learning practices. Students need to be prepared for a digital world, and that includes learning on electronic platforms. That reality will trend stronger every year until it's inextricable from the fabric of the educational landscape. However, this does not mean that technology can, should, or will replace teachers. Technology is a tool, and in that sense laptops and SMART Boards are no different from books and calculators.

That fact is essential to keep in mind as too often technology gets overhyped by parents, school boards, and politicians alike. In the big push for learning environments blended with technology, some people forget the importance of human interaction in education. Technology (at least as of this writing) cannot, on its own, make people smarter. To illustrate this point, consider the following scenarios.

> **Scenario 1:** On a deserted island sits an eight-year-old child at a table with a solar-powered laptop. The laptop is loaded with the best learning software known to humanity. Every nuanced tool for teaching reading, writing, mathematics, language, maintenance, health, and survival is installed onto the system.
>
> **Scenario 2:** On a deserted island sits an eight-year-old child at a table with a twenty-four-year-old third-grade teacher. The teacher was trained with the best educational degree known to humanity. Every nuanced tool for teaching reading, writing, mathematics, language, maintenance, health, and survival was embedded into the teacher's training.

What outcomes would you predict for the child after one year in each scenario?

It's difficult to say definitively which of these scenarios is best. If we're measuring factual knowledge, scenario 1 is very competitive. When considering the child's need to apply learned skills to the real world, though, we'd contend that even endless video tutorials can't match a human teacher. But, there's one more scenario to consider.

> **Scenario 3:** On a deserted island sits an eight-year-old child at a table with a twenty-four-year-old third-grade teacher. The teacher was trained with the best educational degree known to humanity. The teacher has a solar-powered laptop. Every nuanced tool for teaching reading, writing, mathematics, language, maintenance, health, and survival is loaded onto the system.

Clearly, for the best results, you want the best tools *and* a great teacher. You can debate the first two scenarios, but the third is a clear winner.

When it comes to integrating technology, we recommend taking the perspective that learning is learning, no matter whether the work gets done on a laptop or in a notebook. Coupled with great teachers and strong systems, blended learning is just a shift inside the same academic model. Yes, blended learning affords efficiency to teachers as easily as it affords troubling technological distractions. Its expense is handicapping. Its troublesome infrastructure demands are frustrating. But technology is not the educational apocalypse. It's just a tool that needs to be carefully managed, governed, and leveraged for all its worth to help students. The "new toy" excitement and tempting distractions can inhibit progress in a blended classroom. Students working on technology like laptops can appear quiet and compliant on the surface while actually being off task. So, as a leader, it's important to make sure that classroom teachers are actively proctoring (walking around the class and managing engagement) when student technology is used in the classroom. Teachers need to be sure that their students are actively engaged in the right content, at the right time. This is no small task given all of the distractions that come with individual technology. Still, leaders need to insist that, along with technology, teachers use active classroom proctoring, continue their methods of physical reteaching, use benchmarked data requirements, and continually check for understanding.

Guided Practice

After our overview of adjusting for demographic differences, setting up a responsible model for student work expectations focused on classwork and homework, and outlining a direction for blended learning, we want to point out the importance of *guided practice* to the process of teaching students. Guided practice is the interaction between teacher and students wherein the teacher introduces new instruction and then engages students in practicing the same task.

Guided practice expectations will vary in different demographic settings. Some settings may carry heavy homework expectations and come with a high level of parental involvement in the practice component at home. Others may be limited by poor parent involvement and lower homework expectations. That said, both teacher and school leader can ensure there is adequate learning time by providing enough guided practice in the classroom. When considering the influences of home inconsistencies, technology, and blended learning environments, the largest challenge is making sure students are on task with the intended educational assignment, and not just compliantly occupying themselves with other unrelated tasks. Teachers, and ultimately the school leader, need to maintain this kind of guidance over the learning process to make sure engagement is high and learning opportunities are consistent.

As a new leader, or a veteran leader in a new setting, staying connected to the educational process is paramount. It's easy to fill up your time with logistical concerns, fall into the trap of focusing only on what you're good at, lock yourself in your office, and delegate everything away to others. Without regular classroom oversight, you risk the decay of your academic systems. Just like a teacher proctoring guided practice with students in the classroom, the leader must guide the teachers, ensuring the academic and cultural models stay intact.

In a classroom, it takes months of guided practice for the rigor of the process to start showing impact. The same is true for the school leader when observing teachers implementing the school model. It's redundant, but guided practice takes *guidance*. Think back to the deserted island with the eight-year-old child. In scenarios 2 and 3, the child's process was guided by an instructor. In scenario 1, with only the laptop, it was just practice, and any bad habits the child developed would've been allowed to progress in any way the child saw fit. But with guidance, the learning process is more focused, pacing can be controlled, and growth will be more efficient.

If actually *doing* the work is the key to growth, and *interaction* is one of the true keys to education, then guiding that practice with interaction seems like a solid basis for implementation. If it's truly that simple, though, why don't more school leaders do it? The answer is that everything else keeps getting in the way. As we mentioned early on, without a laser focus on strategic systems, we get lost in the process and become too reactive. Remember: we learn by doing, but our teachers grow with guidance.

Summary

In this chapter, we discussed designing and implementing your academic systems. The best way to prevent chaos is to engage students academically, and this idea forms the foundation of effective teaching. Unfortunately, there is great variance in teachers' abilities to engage students, so we recommend creating consistency with a simple, codified model. Your model should define what to teach (a guaranteed and viable curriculum), how to teach it (effective instructional practices), and how it will be monitored (formative and summative assessments). Teachers can and should infuse each of these elements with their own personality and style, but a codified academic system establishes consistent quality throughout the school. Of course, every school and community are different, so we addressed the need for leaders to customize their systems to the needs of their population. In the next chapter, we explore considerations and techniques for managing your staff.

Chapter 6 Reflection Questions

1. How will you and your teachers actively engage students in academics starting from the first day of school?

2. What steps have you taken to ensure there are guaranteed and viable curricula for every grade level and subject area? What is still left to do?

3. In what ways have you clearly defined best practices for instruction and assessment that you expect teachers to incorporate into their lessons? Is there more to be done?

4. Considering the student and parent population you serve, what special considerations for school-home interaction do you and your staff need to account for?

5. Based on your unique student population and school community, do you need to modify your homework practices, use of technology, or other aspects of your academic systems?

CHAPTER 7
Manage Your Staff

While previous chapters have discussed leading the school culture and managing logistics, the fact remains that a school leader is a manager of employees. Managing your staff, both as individuals and as a group, can be difficult, especially when crises arise or hard talks are needed. Regardless of prior experience, stepping in to lead a team (especially one established before your arrival) is an intimidating prospect. However, managing employees is a skill that you can develop or improve, and this chapter provides a number of approaches and strategies.

Managing Your Staff as Individuals

In education, as we've reiterated throughout this book, one size does not fit all. New leaders often want to make a big impact, but many make the mistake of trying to clone themselves. In other words, a new leader who was a highly successful classroom teacher might think, "Now that I'm in charge, I can replicate my success by asking my staff to use the same strategies and style I did." Consider the following story, which exemplifies the thought process of a new leader.

> When I made the move from successful teacher to administrator, I had a solid plan. My classroom instructional style had proven effective. My impact on students was deep and motivating. I knew if I had the proper time and support, I could replicate my instructional style and my tricks of the trade to train a savvy, impactful staff who could all do the same. And then reality hit . . .
>
> My teachers were confused. I was asking them to do things beyond their preparation. They were trying to change everything about their teaching, going off script from their training and past experience. They wanted to impress, and tried as hard as they could, but their personalities and intangible skills did not fit with my strategies. Sure, one or two of them

> found a modicum of success, but in general I had failed. I had tried to clone myself, and it backfired. It was time to quickly re-evaluate and find a solution before I sank the ship.

Consider all the pieces that contribute to effective teaching: implementation model, interaction style, innate responses, planning strategies, the ability to respond when things go off script, attitude, perseverance, and diligence. Even when you codify your academic systems (as described in chapter 6, page 107), each of these elements requires a personal touch. You are the only person in the world who does things the way you do. Sometimes the things that work make no sense at all, but because you're *you*, they just do. Scripting every aspect of teaching or trying to project your individuality onto someone else just does not work.

It's even more destructive to try to apply your personal model to an entire staff or entire system. In doing so, you not only strip the potential for individuality from the process, but you face the risk of systemwide failure when most teachers can't do their best under your constraints. Remember, education is a field that has been researched and tested for hundreds of years. Your surefire strategies are probably less an innovation than a personalization of tried-and-true methods. Your past success was likely very dependent on your personal skill set. In chapter 6 (page 117), we talked about demographic differences and the need to be sensitive to the individuals or communities involved. Your new staff members are no different. Without respecting their individual differences, you're creating a restrictive environment that's bound to fall apart. Instead, you need to leverage your skills, wisdom, and best practices to lift up your staff and support them in achieving their own personal best. Effective leaders help others succeed.

Pause & Reflect

What strategies do you use that might not work for everyone? What are some ways you can provide leadership without assuming your staff will teach like you did?

Managing Your Staff as a Whole

Your teachers will always be your strongest assets. As we've been discussing, they all bring different talents to the workplace. Each of them has exceptional skills as well as areas in need of improvement. Considering the dangers of dictating your personal style to them, you'll find more success approaching staff development by focusing support in a unifying direction. In other words, you need your entire team working together according to your school's model or plan. This can be challenging, as noted author Malcolm Gladwell (2002) sums up in his book *The Tipping Point*: "in order to create one contagious movement, you often have to create many small movements first" (p. 192). To get the whole organization moving in a single direction, many small systems need to cooperate. Navigating individual needs in a way that keeps all staff working toward a common goal is easier when you approach the task through *asset-based management.*

Asset-Based Management

When considering your staff as a whole, each teacher is an asset. While every teacher has individual strengths, we must acknowledge that not every asset brings the same value to the system. From hiring to evaluation to renewal, you need to be able to objectively assess the potential and value of your team. Thinking of your team as assets helps you to invest in individuals when it's worth the effort and let go of individuals when they detract from the larger system. The key aspect of asset-based management is removing personal attachment. When a school leader overprioritizes personal relationships, staff can tell. When leaders let loyalty trump teacher effectiveness, high-performing staff can become disenfranchised, and low-performing staff persist, causing detriments to students. When leaders drive the system via assets and capacity, there are clear expectations for staff, and the system improves over time. In other words, high performance provides the highest value.

To enact asset-based management, you need a simple rating system to compare positives and negatives for every team member. This system needn't be complicated—even a two-factor system that considers the performance data and culture fit of each staff member is sufficient. You can weight these factors as you see fit, perhaps by assigning points for each category. Figure 7.1 (page 132) provides a matrix for evaluating the rating system data.

Consider the following descriptions of each rating shown in figure 7.1.

- **Deficient:** This team member is causing academic harm and pulling down staff culture. Think objectively about whether this person is capable of improving, or if time spent trying to change him or her is merely stealing time from those who could actually benefit from extra attention. Some leaders, recognizing the trouble this staff member is causing, will spend all their time trying to deal with the problem,

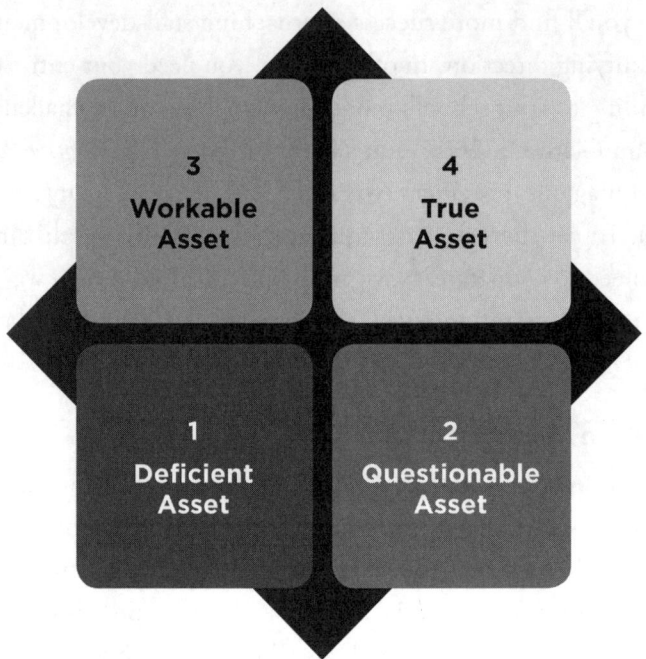

Figure 7.1: Asset-based management matrix.

creating the illusion that this staff member is actually of higher importance. Buffer the negative impact this staff member will have on the organization by finding safe, less critical roles or positions for him or her on staff, but be cautious not to continually fight an unwinnable battle. These individuals need to leave the system or be put in positions that minimize harm.

- **Questionable:** This team member has shown moments of promise and is quick to insist on autonomy. However, he or she regularly deviates from the model without understanding or owning the mistake. This person's failure tends to be cumulative, generating frustration and compounding the negative impact. There is a lack of understanding, buy-in, or true job capacity inhibiting development. Time spent developing this person has immediate impact, but he or she quickly reverts to earlier practices. This person requires constant attention, so gauge the time investment against your leadership team's capacity.

- **Workable:** This team member is a workable asset and continues to make a good impression by showing glimpses of high capacity. Perhaps slow to develop, he or she is a noticeable academic or culture fit on staff who would be tough to replace. Time invested in developing this person is returned with noticeable improvement. Glimpses of leadership potential will likely motivate your attention. This is the most critical staff member for your organization. Growing and retaining teachers in this category are how you make the biggest difference. Allocate most of your staff development time to this segment of the population. Keep these teachers motivated, and make sure they have the support they need to move your organization forward.

- **True:** This team member is an example for the school. He or she has complete model buy-in and backs your leadership with great loyalty. This teacher's performance data and culture contributions set the standard. Staff members in this category hold formal or informal leadership positions and are driven by your trust in their additional responsibilities. While they enjoy additional administrative attention, they are proud of their autonomy, and become great mentors for lower-performing staff. Because these staff members are obvious leaders, they represent program stability. Losing these key members can diminish staff morale and change the balance of the system. Staying tuned in to their needs and concerns is critically important.

For a leader, asset evaluation is an important process that prioritizes the school and the system as a whole and considers staff contributions (or detractions) from that whole. You've created a system that includes cultural norms (chapter 5, page 85), academic systems (chapter 6, page 101), and many other subsystems, so now you're going to allow the system to be the benchmark. That allows you to be objective as you analyze your staff. Once you have an asset-based snapshot of your team, you can start to align your support allocations and future staffing strategies.

When it comes to the makeup of your staff, you will probably have as many strong leaders as you have liabilities, but those two groups represent the extremes of the talent range. In all likelihood, the majority of your staff (perhaps 70 percent; see figure 7.2, page 134) will fall somewhere in between. Some of these will be questionable assets and some workable. Developing your staff then becomes a matter of developing these mid-range teachers. You need your questionable assets to improve, and you need your workable assets to either hold steady or grow. Again, you'll need to protect your true assets at the top of the range so they can sustain and model the system. The staff at the low-questionable or deficient end of the range can then be remediated or removed. If you manage this task well, you can expand the portion of staff creating a positive impact each year and lower the number of staff harming the system. In

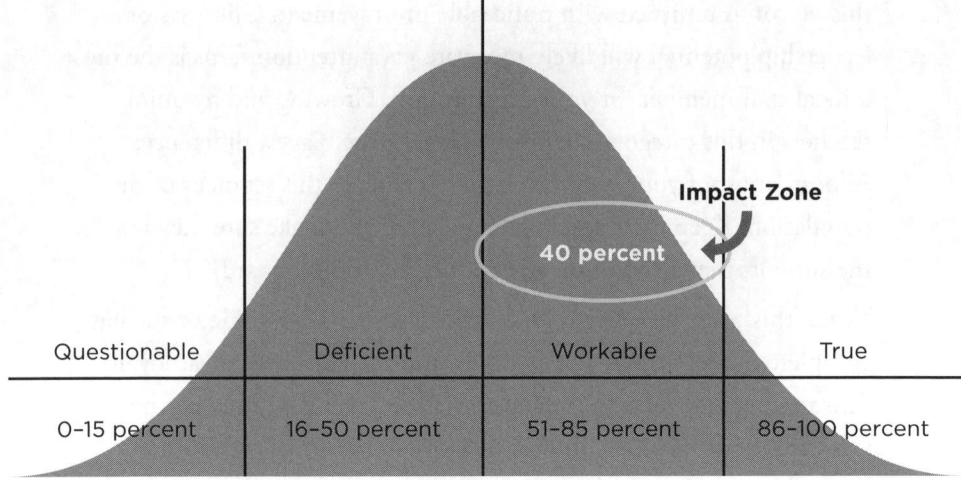

Figure 7.2: Year 1 asset-based staffing map.

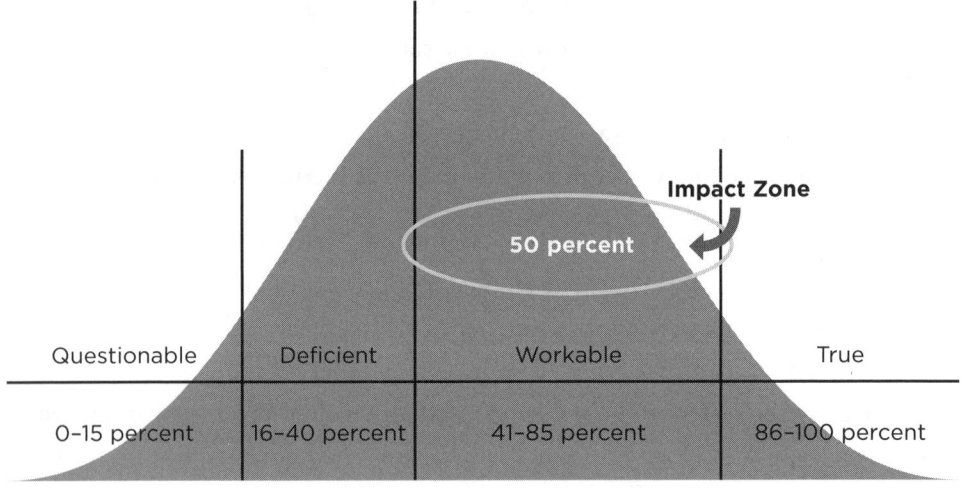

Figure 7.3: Year 2 asset-based staffing map.

other words, if you retain the true assets, strengthen the workable assets, develop any existing questionable assets, and make smart hiring choices to replace any liabilities, your percentage of impactful staff increases (figures 7.3 and 7.4).

The key to this concept is the focus on performance data and culture fit. While this uncomplicated approach allows for simple segmentation of an entire staff, it doesn't impose any grandiose or universal fixes for problems. Instead, it facilitates identification of those who need assistance, and in what capacity. This helps the leader treat each staff member individually, winning smaller targeted battles that move the system forward and help align the organization with its larger goals.

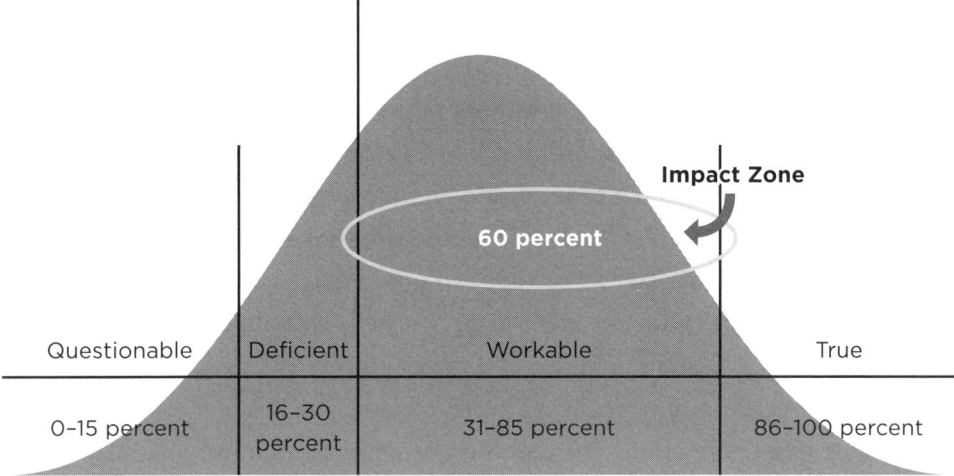

Figure 7.4: Year 3 asset-based staffing map.

It's important to remember that in asset-based management, personal attachment is your most daunting enemy. Guard against favoritism and keep a balanced, objective eye on the development of your staff. In that way, the cumulative effect of a system with growing capacity for impact can take hold.

Objectivity and Performance Data

Now let's take a look at performance data and how you can use such information to objectively guide staff development. This is one of the basic building blocks of a data-driven culture. Think about the following example, which exemplifies how data can drive improvement.

> Our teachers know their numbers. They know their fellow teachers' numbers. They know their number goal, their benchmarked progress toward that goal, and what numbers are needed to be considered effective on staff. Our students also know their own numbers. They know their benchmark targets and attack them like they are in a sporting event. We're all in the same game with the same goals. It's a level playing field from the start with data. We're all fighting to raise the bar, both individually and from class to class, and we celebrate every victory along the way.

Using performance data in this manner changes the relationship between teachers and leaders from something potentially very subjective and emotionally charged to something more concrete. Interpersonal relationships in the workplace are challenging enough, so managing the relationship with concrete benchmarks is critical. This is where data really help.

Student performance data and classroom performance data are static measures of performance not tied to relationships. In a data-driven culture, the performance metric determines the ongoing conversation. In other words, you aren't judging your staff—the data are. You can still provide motivation through praise and supportive accolades, but you don't have to be the "bad guy" when it comes to the need for improvement. Data become the only bad guy on staff. Data do not make subjective decisions. So, if your school's culture defines need, growth, success, or failure through data, your low-performing staff are less likely to blame you for their stresses, failures, transfers, or even terminations. Instead, they must first account for their inability to make gains in their students' academic performance. We're not suggesting that school leaders ignore personal relationships entirely, but a data-driven culture eliminates the subjective issues and informs how we navigate individual relationships.

Too often, a principal finds him- or herself in the unenviable position of responding to a teacher who is not performing well. Consider the following examples of how a leader might navigate this situation.

> **Relationship-based management**
>
> "I know he's struggling academically, but he's just such a great person and everyone likes him. I really enjoy having him on staff. I just need to keep supporting him, and I know he'll get there."

> **Data-based response**
>
> "In a year's work, he hasn't been able to move his class above the 40th percentile in math, but his language arts scores are in the 70th percentile. I've got to get him the help he needs in number sense and get him working with our higher-performing math teachers."

Both scenarios represent struggling teachers needing the school leader's individual attention. In the first example, the leader's feedback lacks objective, measurable goals. Instead, it's a message of support, intent, and inspiration. It's also likely to leverage a strong personal bond between teacher and leader to inspire future performance. Unfortunately, it conveys no plan for future success outside of goodwill and optimism. It's a classic case of, "You're awesome, so try harder, OK?" If you leave this struggling teacher to himself without a managed path to improvement, he'll either seek direction elsewhere, which can put his success beyond your control, or fail to find a viable path to improvement and continue to underperform.

In the second scenario, you see a data-driven approach to improvement. This is where data are a wonderful tool. Student performance scores (in this case) create specificity. The leader defines the problem clearly and identifies a solution. The response is still supportive and even optimistic, but it's also practical. The teacher whose leader uses a data-based response has a much better chance of improving.

We're not trying to downplay the importance of emotional intelligence, relationships, or culture fit. Those aspects of your educational environment are essential, too, but they do not provide benchmarks for managing and developing teachers. If you establish a system based on data with a focus on developing your teacher assets, you're setting the tone for how your culture will develop around those expectations. That way, you've laid a foundation from which your new school's culture can grow. From that base, staff relationships have common ground and are less divisive.

Balance and the Ongoing Hiring Process

Just as we recommended performance and culture fit as two factors for assessing individual teachers, you'll also want to consider using these metrics to evaluate the balance of your entire staff. Each staff member on your team needs to perform well and fit into the school culture, but some people contribute more overall to the culture and others primarily contribute their instructional prowess. Your staff need to have a balance of these characteristics. You need to balance your culture contributors, who exemplify the communication and behavioral expectations at school, and performance contributors, who exemplify the data-driven and academic performance expectations at school. Unfortunately, the human dynamic is unique, and this often means you'll be facing a new staff that have a variable group of both culture contributors and performance contributors. Consider the sweet spot in the chart in figure 7.5 (page 138). As a leader, you ideally want to maintain a fairly even ratio of performance-driven talent to culture-driven talent. Outside of a 60–40 percent split on either side, your systems are likely to suffer.

This chart tells us that it's both appropriate and necessary to hire people who will add value to both culture and performance. A school that is too heavy with culture contributors may feel very warm and welcoming with a very tightly bonded staff, but the focus on systems and academic processes will eventually erode, taking a back seat

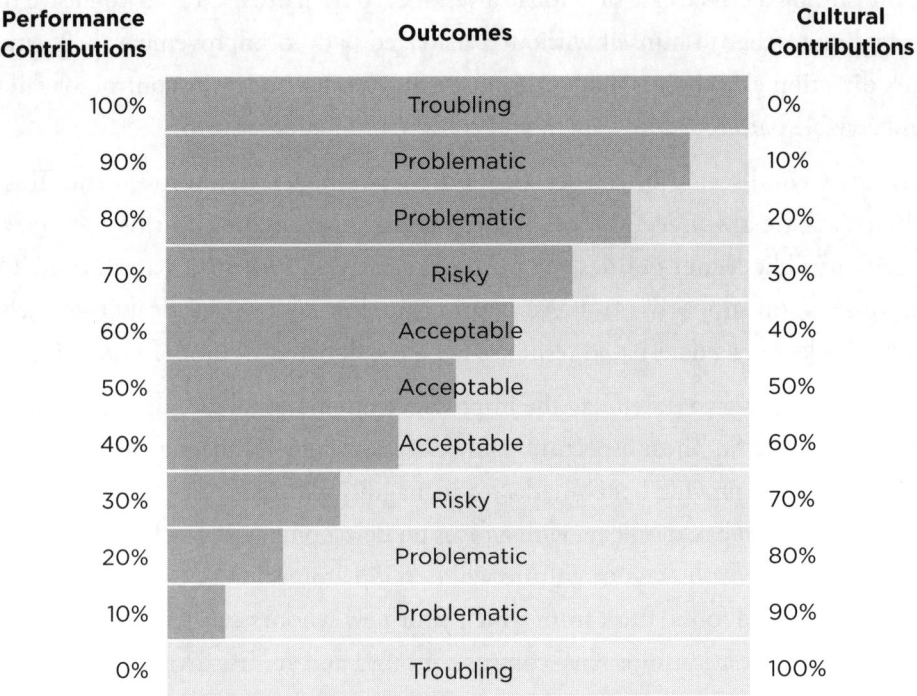

Figure 7.5: The balance of culture and performance in staffing.

to the school atmosphere. The inverse is also troubling. Too much focus on performance can create a school that sees results and outcomes as the only measure of success. While these schools can show substantial early growth, the intensity of the effort can lead to burnout and turnover. This instability will eventually erode the school's academic gains as it has to replace and retrain staff. Whether your particular school model leans more to culture or more to academic outcomes, the need for balance is the same. Avoiding extremes in the hiring process and looking for a blend or fairly balanced set of belief systems is a great starting point for the interview process. This mindset can also help guide the formation of balance-specific interview questions for prospective staff candidates.

As a new leader or veteran in a new setting, hiring a well-balanced staff is important at the onset, but it's hard to accomplish when you're new to a school. The long game of hiring takes consecutive years and requires a great deal of patience. The teaching market may ebb and flow over the years, but one constant will always remain: good teachers are hard to replace. Good teachers who leave your system can diminish performance and sabotage your culture. Once you have a balance of talent, making sure you keep that talent is key to your success. The best school leaders typically have the best teachers, and therein lies one of the inherent gifts of good leaders—they know how to retain talent.

Start this process early by identifying and keying into your staff leaders. We explained this concept in chapter 1 (page 23) as we discussed key stakeholders. As a new leader, you'll need to know who your quality leaders are by meeting with staff immediately and analyzing your assets. You have to spend quality time with your leaders, working to understand what their needs are and creating systems to support them. Staff retention programs and workplace incentives will give you a better chance at keeping top talent in place. Lastly, it's important to remember that, despite your best efforts, your initial staff may turn over in three to four years, especially in small schools, independent schools, and brand-new settings. Build for today, but plan for tomorrow. Your first few new hires may or may not become your long-term mainstays. Consider the following story.

> I've been involved in public, private, and charter schools since 1995. In that time, I've lived through the startup of five different schools. The one constant I have found in terms of staffing a new school from scratch is that the initial staff will begin to turn over in the third year. By year six or seven, you've likely turned over a majority of the starting staff. It's not a rule to live by, but it's a fact to grapple with. The culture shift that unwinds after a new start can be a dramatic change because the idealistic culture aspired to on day one gets overwritten by adjustments to the real world. This shift will take its toll on a staff, and it's not necessarily a bad thing.
>
> The second phase of staffing, arriving after the culture shift, may well be the glue that holds the evolved system together. These new team members' expectations at the time of hire will be better aligned with the realities of the growing system.
>
> Good leaders shouldn't consider initial hires as wasted value but should have the strength to endure the turnover when an evolving school begins to move beyond some of the original staff.

Staff turnover will be a reality for new leaders in any school, but especially in brand-new schools. It's extremely hard to find success when incorporating a litany of new systems in any setting. With the realities of new systems, new expectations, new students, new parents, a new neighborhood, a new commute, and so on, a segment of your staff population will feel like they have jumped into the deep end and can't swim. Self-selection out of that situation is an ongoing reality.

By year 2 in your new setting, you'll likely have seen self-selection or terminations cull some of your lower-performing teachers. Those who remain may be settling in and getting a good feel for the system, or they may be hanging by a thread. By year 3, you'll lose another small percentage of low performers, but high performers from your original staff also begin to analyze the setting. They have streamlined their classroom processes and are starting to look up from time to time and notice that the school they signed up for has begun to evolve. This evolution may or may not be what they expected. In this moment, even your best teachers may begin to question whether they want to stay the course. Occasionally, great teachers will resist the evolution of the program and openly challenge the administration. In such an unfortunate situation, great teachers who are no longer a great fit must be let go. Your school will be better for it.

The moral of the story here is to stay objective, finding a safe balance between culture contributors and performance contributors. Strong systems take time to build, and a balanced staff will smooth the bumps over the initial years. Remember that larger gains are won through many smaller gains. Those smaller victories are individual to every member of your staff. Learn to develop strong individual relationships with your staff to aid in the smaller goals, but analyze those wins objectively with benchmarks and measurable data. Manage academic gaps and make sure you set a high bar in a data-driven culture.

Responding to Difficult Situations

Another challenging but critical aspect of managing your staff is responding to difficult situations. New leaders often struggle in this area. No one likes confrontation or awkward conversations with underperforming teachers, and it takes time to develop the confidence and experience to respond capably. To give you an advantage, we provide guidance on initiating hard conversations, dousing fires, and navigating stress and confrontation.

Initiating Hard Conversations

Even though you have established cultural norms and codified your academic systems, you'll find that no matter how many times you reinforce them, some people just won't get the point. No need to panic—this happens to every leader. Remember, you must overcome many smaller issues before the larger movement can take hold and proliferate. This applies in culture, norms, and staff behavior.

When certain individuals aren't getting the message, you can't be afraid of difficult conversations. Hard talks are important but initially stressful for all involved. These conversations are most effective when they get to the point quickly and offer succinct pathways for improvement. They need to be held in private, balanced with support and personalized care, and founded on a clear intention for improvement. You can use the following three-step format to guide difficult conversations.

1. **Acknowledgment of a meaningful role in the organization:** "Your presence here at _____ has made a real difference. We love having you on staff."

2. **Measurable change directive:** "But listen, you've violated our communication frameworks multiple times this week, and it's become a problem. In the coming week, let's both monitor your communication to see if we can go a week without any issues. We can meet at the same time next week and discuss how it went."

3. **Caring closing statement:** "I want you to know we care about you and want to support what you bring to the school, so let's tackle this together and get on top of it. I'll follow up with an email confirming what we talked about and send you a calendar invite for our next meeting."

This is a classic "support sandwich" approach, in which you bookend the tough message with supportive ones. A leader could insert any ongoing issue into the second step and conduct the same meeting. The main thing to remember here is to keep things concise so the conversation can remain tactful and easy to document. Don't get carried away with step 1 and step 3—expounding on a litany of positives can bury the intended message. The focus of the meeting is step 2, so keep the sandwich simple. Ideally, it's done in a few minutes, and the singular focus for improvement is clear. Note the mention in step 3 about following up with an email. This cements the conversation into written record. Should a problem escalate, documentation of these conversations will show your diligence in addressing the issue. Or, should the staff member say he or she didn't know or didn't understand, you've got a record to help reset the conversation.

Unfortunately, one hard talk with your staff doesn't typically solve all underlying issues. Like anything else in education, one attempt at change is usually insufficient. And, like everything else in human nature, everyone will respond differently to a hard talk. Recall the four basic categories of teacher ratings from an earlier section (page 131). To some extent, you can also predict a teacher's reaction to a hard talk based on these ratings. For example, your true assets will take ownership of problems you bring to their attention. They are likely extremely self-aware, stressed by the conversation, and unwilling to endure the personal shame of further hard talks. They will get the message loud and clear and won't need further redirection.

The majority of your staff—your workable and questionable assets—will likely need multiple redirections. This brings us to our *theory of nine*. With this theory, we set leaders up for patience through the process of redirection and mentoring by keeping the focus on the long game of coaching. More specifically, if you accept that it may take as many as nine hard talks before key messages take hold, you're less likely to get upset at the constant redirects. It's a simple worst-case assumption. If you work under the knowledge that you'll have to repeat yourself multiple times before someone truly gets your message, you'll lower your frustrations through the process. Your continual hard talks will push your staff to their capacity, but they will make progress. Typically, the higher a staff member is on your internal asset-based scale, the fewer redirects he or she will need; questionable assets may need regular conversations throughout the year just to stay on track. This lower subgroup often responds positively to redirects, but then quickly reverts back to old habits.

Finally, we have our deficient assets. Some of these staff will need to move on, finding places that are better suited to their abilities and temperaments. It can be challenging, for both practical and interpersonal reasons, to build a case for a struggling staff member's removal. With the theory of nine, though, the process is normed. You've committed to addressing issues when they arise, and you follow a consistent step-by-step, documented approach, regardless of the teacher's usual performance level. The theory of nine allows for numerous documented redirects, each one key to establishing a plan for improvement, transfer, resignation, or termination. See figure 7.6.

Challenge Zone Questionable and Deficient Assets	**Impact Zone** Workable Assets	**Performance Zone** True Assets
• Needs regular hard talks • Reverts to subpar norms	• Needs multiple redirects • Requires patience • Produces in the end	• Self-sustaining • Takes ownership • Self-aware

Figure 7.6: Theory-of-nine zones.

Applied to your whole staff, the theory of nine becomes a cultural norm. Over time, your staff will understand that these conversations aren't threatening. They happen in a safe, supportive space and become part of the feedback, support, and growth process. Your authentic pursuit of improvement for teachers and your use of the support sandwich will grow individual relationships. You'll demonstrate patience and leadership as you willingly tackle issues up to nine times. Of course, you must maintain that threshold; expecting nine redirects only to lose your patience and give up after three will damage your rapport with staff. You might choose a different number as your target, but this approach reinforces high expectations and continuous improvement.

It is important to note that failing to address a teacher's deviation from culture norms or performance expectations causes widespread damage. Ignoring a problem communicates to other staff that underperformance is acceptable. Inaction equals approval. Inconsistency is just as damaging; you can't enforce norms one day only to lose momentum and stop enforcing them later. As a leader, don't allow an unmanaged norm to redefine your school culture. Utilize the theory of nine or a similar approach to lock in and model the importance of patient, consistent redirections and high expectations.

Dousing Fires

There are many days as a school leader when you might feel the title of *firefighter* is more appropriate than *principal*. You're not alone. The fires or urgent situations that new principals face tend to fall into four categories: (1) high job demands with unreasonable expectations, (2) managing difficult stakeholders, (3) problematic work-life balance, and (4) lack of support (De Jong, Grundmeyer, & Yankey, 2017). In the initial days, this barrage of stress can be very overwhelming. All staff, parents, and students will be looking to you as the chief leader in the building for answers and decisions on everything. Moreover, everyone will want a few minutes with you as the new principal to push his or her own agenda or request. Remind yourself that not every fire is necessarily a true inferno. Prioritizing fires must become a daily ritual. There is a delicate balance between making people feel heard and allowing nonessential tasks to monopolize your precious time, so keep your leadership priorities in check. Always remember that the key priorities when choosing which fire to fight are (1) safety of staff and students and (2) the education of students. While other fires may want your attention, when juxtaposed against safety or education, prioritize accordingly.

Navigating Stress and Confrontation

Throughout this section, we've been talking about what to do when things get tough. Here, we discuss your response to confrontation and other stressful situations. How you handle stress will define your tenure at your school. When you boil it down to the basic elements, we typically hear about two common responses to stress: fight or flight. But, we suggest that there are four options in any stressful situation: fight, fix, freeze, or flight.

Each of these responses to confrontation and stress has inherent positive and negative attributes depending on how it's applied. In his book, *The Science of Fear*, psychology writer Daniel Gardner (2009) illustrates how our fear causes problems when we miscalculate risk with our instinctive and reactive hunter-gatherer brains. In other words, sometimes our gut reactions lead us astray. So, while fight and flight can save our lives, those instinctive tools are typically only positive in the context of basic human responses to imminent danger—they are reactionary, life-preserving actions. But, when used strategically, the concept of fight or flight moves from a life-saving effort to something more intentionally negative. For example, strategic decisions to fight look like bullying, and strategic flight tends to look more like avoidance.

The remaining two responses, fix and freeze, are much more effective tools for responding to the stressful but non-life-threatening situations you'll encounter as a school leader. But, they are nuanced terms, each very closely relating to the other. What differentiates the two is how quickly a fix can or should be applied to the problem. For instance, if the initial response to stress was to try and immediately fix the problem, that quick reaction may cause other problems that compound the stress. This is what we call a reactive fix. In other words, trying to fix a problem reactively can offend or shame someone. A strategic fix, on the other hand, can solve the immediate issue, but only after it has been determined that no further harm would come from the solution. In this way, the word *proactive* means consciously deciding to act after evaluating the scenario (making a determination that minimal harm will be done by engaging in the fix).

Freeze functions similarly to fix. Reactively, a freeze can inhibit action when action is needed. This is the concept of being frozen with fear (Roelofs, Hagenaars, & Stins, 2010). But strategically, a freeze (a conscious decision to either disengage, hold back a response, or inhibit your action) can become one of the most useful tools in your arsenal. Consider table 7.1, which summarizes the results of each response in different situations.

Table 7.1: The Impact of Fight, Fix, Freeze, and Flight Responses

	Reactive	Strategic
Fight	Life saving	Bullying
Fix	Problem generating	Problem solving
Freeze	Problem generating	Problem solving
Flight	Life saving	Avoidance

Outside of a dire emergency, fight and flight responses are probably too extreme for any workplace. When responding to a stressful situation, your best options are fix and freeze, which we describe in more detail in the following sections.

The Fix

In some stressful yet non-life-threatening situations, the best response is simply to fix the problem. If the problem is obvious and a solution can be applied without harming yourself or others, just fix it (strategic). Consider the following story from the perspective of a school leader who applied a strategic fix.

> **Lunchroom Panic**
>
> I heard a call over the radio from my dean asking for a janitorial cleanup in the cafeteria. There was some urgency to his voice, so I knew he had a mess on his hands. A couple minutes later, another call came through, and then another, all asking for janitorial. I was in a meeting and couldn't step away to look into the situation, but then the dean showed up at my door. He was obviously reactively frozen (didn't know what to do) and very upset. Excusing myself, I stepped into the hall to meet him, and he proceeded to explain, with large animated gestures, how a third grader had vomited during lunch and another had then sympathy-vomited next to him. The smell was horrible, the vomit puddle was blocking the tray-return line, and he couldn't find the janitors. The kids at lunch were making a huge deal about it and going crazy. Nobody could empty their trays, and the next lunch rotation was already coming in.
>
> I asked my office guest to give me five minutes and told the dean to follow me. I went to the janitorial closet, grabbed the bucket and mop, and walked downstairs to the cafeteria. I didn't say anything, but I knew this was a strategic fix that I could model. I mopped up the puke, then scooted the mop

and bucket to the side and motioned for the dean to continue lunch. He got a kick out of seeing me playing janitor, and things went back to normal.

For the dean, the shock of the situation coupled with the lack of a janitor had blocked his ability to think clearly. In that stress, it didn't occur to him to just assess the issue, stay strategic, fix the problem, and clean up the mess himself. He had frozen, and calling for help was the only solution he could think of. I was back in my office with the problem resolved within five minutes.

So, while strategically fixing the problem may seem like the easy solution, sometimes we are blinded by stress or chaos. In these moments, we all need the help and support of those around us. Still, the rule for a great strategic fix is no different from the rule in a first-aid situation: always make sure that you won't do further harm and that the scene is safe before you try to fix it yourself. To be clear, *harm* in this context isn't always physical. For instance, if you act reactively (without thinking it through) and fix a problem for a teacher in front of other teachers, then you could risk shaming the teacher in front of his or her peers. In terms of safety, some situations require that you call in someone who is better equipped. But if the situation is safe and the solution harmless, you can step in, be strategic, and make things right. Here's another example.

In the Dark

The power for the entire school went out in a flash. The facility manager came running into the office in a panic, her cell phone light guiding her way. Not seeing me, she ran straight to the secretary and said, "Get on the phone to the power company right now! Get them out here ASAP!"

I flashed my own cell phone light her way and motioned for her to come over to me. Reassuring the office staff, I said, "We'll likely need that call, but hold the thought until we return." I led the facility manager down to the basement, and we made our way to the main breaker. The lever was in the down position; it had tripped. Asking the facility manager to shine her light toward it, I walked over and leaned into the power box to flip the breaker back up.

With a huge metallic clang, the large breaker popped back up, and the building whirred back to life. The facility manager and I walked back up to the office where business was already back to normal.

In this story, the facility manager wasn't ready to meet the crisis with the simplest answer. Stress can make it hard to rationalize the best path forward, often incapacitating us and compounding the problem.

All that said, it's often our pride that obscures the best solution during a stressful event. In the first story, the dean didn't consider the strategic fix (lowering himself to the role of "puke cleaner"), and in the next story, the facility manager didn't think to do any more than call the power company, but in both cases, the school leaders strategically modeled a fix for both of them. You see, as a school leader, swallowing pride for the sake of the staff or school is often a daily process. Going beyond your job title and description can feel demoralizing or belittling, but a leader should be willing to take on any role in his or her organization to help fix a break in the system. Accepting that responsibility can keep you cool under pressure, allowing you to see the strategic fix where others might reactively freeze. Great leaders bear the brunt of tough situations so their staff and students don't have to. They model doing what it takes to move forward, even if it involves going beyond the job description.

The Freeze

Sometimes fixing the problem is clear-cut, but in some situations, trying to fix a problem right away might only create more problems. We've explained the downside of a reactive fix, but sometimes a strategic fix is still too risky. In these moments, a freeze is often your most powerful tool as a leader. And, strategically freezing, stopping, or de-escalating a situation is very different from reactively freezing up when you should act. When used as a tactic, the freeze is an essential part of the job. Consider the following seven scenarios in which you can use the freeze.

1. **Upset parents:** An upset parent storms into the office. Her child has just been suspended. She's not calm and not rational. She's verbally tearing into any staff member she can find. In this case, there's no simple solution for the parent. She is hurt, upset, and confused. More than anything, she probably needs to vent and to be heard. The best thing to do is become the target for this parent. Accepting the onslaught, you can save others from the wrath. Usher such a parent into a private space and let her talk (or yell) at you. If you're nervous about the parent's behavior, invite another administrator into the meeting. You don't have to solve this parent's problems, but it's important to validate her. Use phrases like "I can see you're upset," "I can hear the passion in your voice," or "I have a lot of respect for any parent that advocates so strongly for her child." These are strategic

freeze tactics. You're holding your stance on the decisions made—not fixing the problem, but affirming the emotions of the parent. Sometimes, this is a marvelous diffuser. Other times, it leads to a more civil discussion. But, stay strategic. Don't argue with the parent or attempt to rationalize the issue; this will only escalate the situation.

2. **Irrational arguments:** Trying to rationalize an irrational situation is usually a disaster. If you're trapped in an irrational or circular argument, you need to freeze the conversation. This is where approaches like *love and logic* (Fay & Fay, 2012) come into play. Love and logic, a philosophical approach to communication and conflict, employs practical tools and techniques that help adults avoid stressful and chaotic outcomes. From this approach, we find solutions to irrational arguments with empathetic phrases like "I care about your child too much to argue" or "I'm sorry, but I'm not going to argue with you" said over and over work as a brick wall response. This is another great freeze tactic to indicate there is no fix, but also no more room to move in the discussion. It typically helps to stalemate the momentum. While people on the receiving end may not like the approach, it's very effective in bringing an argument to a close without anyone losing face.

3. **Verbal confrontations:** There will be times when the insult or barrage of opinions is so heavy that a calm, controlled, interested expression is all a leader can provide. All confrontation is born out of frustration, and venting is one of the most helpful remedies. Understand that taking on the role of the listener, no matter how foul, hurtful, or accusatory the confrontation, might be the best path forward. Responding with "thank you" or "I hear you" may be the best you can do.

4. **Staff infractions:** A staff member has committed an atrocious violation of school policy. You're fuming. You want to call her into the office and let her know exactly how serious this infraction is and how it will affect the school and her career. As you likely know, it's never wise to address your staff hotheaded. This is a strategic freeze moment. Stop yourself and set a meeting for later in the day or early the next day. This same idea applies to email. Never send an angry email. Take some time to process and collect your thoughts. You're too ready to fight, and you'll generate a fight or flight response from your staff member if you address her now.

5. **Instructional support:** You're observing a teacher who is struggling during instruction. You can see the classroom order starting to devolve as a result. You know how to fix the issue. But, unless students are at risk, this is still a strategic freeze moment. Correcting the teacher in front of the students could compromise his authority. Hold the thought and meet with the teacher immediately after class. Providing the feedback after the fact preserves respect. This also applies in large staff gatherings and group parent interactions. In all these cases, it's important to preserve an individual's integrity. Sometimes that involves allowing an obvious mistake to happen, even if you have the means to reactively fix it in the moment.

6. **Freedom to fail:** You've delegated some management task to your staff, and you see a potential train wreck developing. You know if you step in, you can restore balance and stop a bad situation from happening. Just as in the last case, unless there is imminent danger to students or staff in the looming train wreck, you must remember that we all learn by doing, and life's roadblocks are powerful teachers. That's not to say you should set your staff up to fail, but sometimes you need to give your staff the freedom to fail. It's a subtle but meaningful difference. Facing their own freedom to fail, they will often trip themselves up, but they'll also surprise you with their ingenuity and resilience once they meet your predicted roadblocks. If you always swoop in to save the situation, you're likely reducing your staff's independence and slowing their growth. Stay tuned in, monitoring the situation from an arm's reach—be available, but don't take over. Either through thoughtful coaching as a debrief after the fact, or as a supportive advisor (if consulted) through the situation, you can use this form of a strategic freeze to allow your staff to safely field-test their skills.

7. **Choose to lose:** You've given your staff the freedom to fail, but what about yourself? An example from film is illustrative here. In *Star Wars: Episode IV—A New Hope* (Kurtz & Lucas, 1977), R2-D2 is about to beat Chewbacca in Dejarik, a type of holographic chess, but Han Solo convinces R2 that the droid wouldn't want to face the wrath of a defeated Wookiee, so he lets the Wookiee win (choosing freeze over fix). That's a powerful analogy for school leaders when dealing with personal entitlement or tough staff or parent confrontations. Winning an argument or getting the last word may be tempting, but may not

accomplish anything more than inflaming the situation. Sometimes choosing to lose is the appropriate way to diffuse or de-escalate a challenging problem, though it rarely feels good in the moment. This is also referred to as "falling on the sword" or "taking one for the team," and it's something that great leaders learn to do.

In all these situations and others that may call for a freeze, the overarching rules are *patience* and *validation*. Many of the leader responses in the preceding list illustrate this in a simple context. The first step is to stay calm. Then, patiently assess the appropriate freeze strategy, and validate the stressed party whenever possible. Phrases like "I can see this means a great deal to you" or "I'm impressed by how much you care about your child" legitimize the person's concerns without escalating the tension. Stress and confrontation are all results of frustration, which in turn is the buildup of internalized guilt, anger, confusion, or fear. A teacher, parent, or student feeling those emotions needs to vent, and you need to let him or her do so. There is no perfect solution for these confrontations, but patience and validation will always put you in a position for the best outcome. And, remember—when confrontation and stress seem overwhelming despite your best efforts, you also need to vent! Don't vent in the moment, but don't internalize your stress without a way to deal with it; find a safe outlet away from work and get things off your chest. Often our mentors, parents, and spouses are great outlets for this. Also, consider utilizing a counselor as an outlet. With a personal counselor, your conversations are confidential, but you have the freedom to work through the emotional baggage you are so often forced to carry for your team.

> **Pause & Reflect**
>
> Recall the last few stressful work-related encounters where you were directly involved. Were you strategic or reactive in your role? How might you handle the situation differently in the future?
>
> Consider the concept of giving your staff the freedom to fail. In your role as mentor and leader, how can you apply this to the workplace?

Summary

In this chapter, we shared some wisdom related to one of the biggest challenges a new leader faces: managing staff. Your aim is to strike a balance between positive relationships and objective leadership. Teachers will be most successful if you allow them individuality within your school's codified system, but you must also consider your staff as a whole. Guided by data, the unbiased perspective of asset-based management will help you build a strong, balanced team of educators who contribute to the school's performance and culture. In addition to day-to-day supervision, you'll also need to respond to difficult situations. Tough talks with struggling teachers, various fires that vie for your attention, and stressful or confrontational events all require a calm, supportive approach. In the next chapter, we review some tips for administering your budget.

Chapter 7 Reflection Questions

1. Should you mandate that all teachers use the classroom strategies that were most effective for you? Why or why not?

2. From hiring to evaluation to renewal, how will you objectively assess the potential of your team?

3. Describe asset-based management. How can you use this perspective to drive staff development?

4. How does a data-driven culture change the relationship between leader and staff? How can this type of culture drive your staff performance?

5. What is the best way to structure a difficult conversation? What other guidelines should you follow when delivering corrective feedback?

6. Describe fixing and freezing as responses to stress and confrontation. Why are these strategies effective?

CHAPTER 8

Administer Your Budget

As the new leader in a school, you may not have created the budget for your first year, but you certainly have important responsibilities in this arena. By midway through your initial year, you've likely come to understand some of your school's budgetary realities. Whether you felt prepared for managing your budget or not, you have a large role to play in the outcome of your expenses. When it comes time to budget for your second year, you probably have some ability to dictate or request some of the budgetary needs.

It's nearly impossible to overstate the importance of your budget responsibilities. Outside of legal trouble, there are only two things that typically lead to a school leader losing his or her job: (1) poor academics and (2) poor financial management. When you break down all the mandates within the four walls of your school, academics and finance will play a role in just about everything you do. While educational leadership programs appropriately devote substantial course time to the countless approaches to finding and maintaining academic success, we find that school leaders may not receive much preparation when it comes to school finance. You do not need to be an accountant or a mathematician to navigate finance, though. In this chapter, we cover the basics of budget boundaries, approaches to planning and spending, rough calculations, federal grants, and other sources of supplemental funding.

Budget Boundaries

The first step in financial planning is knowing your boundaries. In your first year, you've likely been handed a budget. This is your first boundary. If you exceed that budget, your job is in jeopardy. If you stay under budget, you'll earn points with the district or board. Unfortunately, things only get more complex from there.

The next boundary to understand is the often-convoluted process for allocating and spending your money. This will vary depending on your setting and local policies. In many large traditional public districts, things can seem fairly oppressive. You have a budget, but you feel like you aren't allowed to spend it on anything without someone else's approval. Central office approvals will slow your timelines. Hiring rules and human resources regulations will reduce your ability to bring on key staff in a timely manner. Since you are effectively a tenant in a district-owned building, facilities improvements are largely out of your control. You may have managerial oversight, but your budget is not designed for implementing changes to the physical plant, traffic flow, landscaping, HVAC system, or security systems. You may have no ability to upgrade Wi-Fi, laptops, or phones. Sometimes, even classroom-level supplies must receive approvals beyond your control.

There is a positive side to this situation, though. If the budget is restricted and you have little latitude to stray from the dollars allocated to your building's needs, then you've had a giant diversion removed from your daily focus. If you had to manage Wi-Fi, landscaping, air-conditioning, laptops, phones, hiring, and classroom supplies on top of your normal responsibilities, you could end up never leaving your office. Those distractions could bury your ability to focus on the important tasks of growing culture, developing teachers, and educating students.

> **Pause & Reflect**
>
> Do you have a clear understanding of your role in managing the school's budget? Do you know which funds are really in your control and which are not?

The key to navigating the budget in these settings is understanding the boundary between your direct control over funds and the central office's control over funds. You can only effect change with what's in your control, so you have to know which funds are yours to manipulate and how to manipulate them. Even in a large district where you have little control, you should track your own budget on the side. The district may have a tracking tool it provides to you, but the point here is not to wait for district reports. The school budget is your budget whether you control every line item or not.

Overstepping budgetary boundaries inevitably results in a disgruntled district team or a talk with the superintendent. In order to navigate this path correctly, you need to know who approves each request for expenditure. Every large-scale academic setting will have department-head-driven pipelines for expenses and approvals in various categories. Their funding allocations will be a direct reflection of the mission and vision of the entire corporation. Understanding the chain of command and overarching vision in these areas will allow you to act in the appropriate frame of mind, which can then speed up your approval process. We recommend keeping a list of the contact person for each department or type of expense. That list of key contacts should include instruction, health and safety, food services, and so on. The appendix (page 183) provides a reproducible contact list you can fill out and keep on hand.

Let's shift to private and charter school models. In these typically smaller settings (and others where the principal has direct responsibility for finances), the budgets are tighter, and every dollar carries significantly more stress—the dollars themselves become your boundaries. As a new leader in this setting, you've likely been handed a budget by a board that expects you to be the final word for expense approvals. If you're leading a brand-new school, you may even have had a hand in developing the initial budget. Either way, this little budget is a ton of responsibility and presents an immense risk to the security of your position. In these settings, budgeting is a dynamic, day-to-day process, dependent on enrollment and fundraising. Tracking your own budget will be more of a central responsibility than for principals in public schools, and much depends on your ability to keep clear and organized track of expenses and expenditures.

Whether you're in a public, private, or charter setting, don't ever mentally allocate, promise, or spend a dollar of organizational money without knowing you have it to spend. You won't be able to accomplish this without some personal accounting on your end. The golden rule here is that academics and finance are the two most powerful levers in education. You can use the lever of finance to lift you and your school to success if you're on top of your own budget.

Approaches to Planning and Spending

Once you understand your budget boundaries, you can take a closer look at planning and spending within those constraints. Here, we discuss three approaches: (1) dynamic budgeting, (2) conservative budgeting, and (3) use-it-or-lose-it spending.

Dynamic Budgeting

In smaller settings, budgets constantly fluctuate. They still operate similarly to larger budgets, but the estimates often suffer from volatility due to the smaller size of the student and staff population. For instance, a school corporation with thirty schools can absorb a 20 percent decline in enrollment at a single site by adjusting funds from the enrollment of all thirty schools. In contrast, a small rural district, a single-site school, or a private organization has little ability to absorb large enrollment losses or facility issues without eliminating programs or making significant cuts to staffing.

Enrollment is always going to be the key factor in dynamic budgeting. We're all pressured to have a full school because all schools receive income based on enrollment, but assuming and budgeting for a full school is very similar to gambling. Estimate too much enrollment, and you're in trouble. Estimate less enrollment, and you'll have more money. Full classrooms are the goal, but they aren't guaranteed. Consider the following example.

> In my first year as a principal, we missed our budgeted enrollment projections by 125 students. We were a brand-new school in a single-site system, and I had to let three staff members go during the first month to offset the loss of revenue. There was nothing I could do. We hired staff for too many kids, and folks lost their jobs when enrollment came up short. It was awful.

With that in mind, school leaders who have the ability to budget for underenrollment (in essence, plan for less income) find themselves in a solid place. Such strategic lowballing dramatically raises the likelihood that the budgeted funding will arrive, even if it's less than you'd like. In other words, plan to have fewer students and less money, and be happy when you get more of both. Conversely, never plan to have more, because folks will be out of a job if you don't get what you predicted.

These smaller sites must be nimble with the budget as realities dictate changes in the flow of income. Their leaders can't approach these systems by holding to their budget as absolute guidelines. Instead, a conservative approach is needed to build reserve cash and to ensure the programs and staffing are protected from unforeseen financial cliffs.

Conservative Budgeting

Conservative budgeting can cause pain up front, and is a philosophy better applied to school leaders with local control over the annual budget. This budgeting methodology means you're intentionally planning to have fewer resources, less income from dependable resources, and perhaps fewer people on staff. It also means you might be trimming the fat (extracurriculars and other nonessential elements) out of your program during the budgeting process. But don't let that scare you. As a new leader in your building, you won't have time for those matters until everything else begins to stabilize. Let the conservative budget guide your focus to what's critically important and what's expendable. The goal is to leave your organization with money in the bank at the end of the budget cycle.

By assuming underenrollment and underestimating your expected income, you've safely protected yourself from an enrollment flop or other income shortfalls. Then, should enrollment exceed expectation, you're in a position to purchase and allocate additional resources to meet the higher demand. That may mean hiring teachers after the first day of school when the talent pool has less to offer, but it also means you're not firing teachers because you missed enrollment. Those leftover dollars represent your ability to be flexible and creative and can put the organization in an enviable cash position in three to five years. Figure 8.1 shows an example of small school in Indiana as it grew from 369 students in its inaugural year to 650 by year five. Note the cash retained at the end of each year.

Year	Beginning Cash Balance	Ending Cash Balance
1	$94,317	$115,982
2	$115,982	$395,730
3	$395,730	$668,217
4	$668,217	$838,919
5	$838,919	$1,024,487

Figure 8.1: Increasing cash balance over five years.

This chart is an approximation from a small local school intent on growing a million-dollar cash reserve. Using a conservative approach, the school hit its goal in its fifth year. Seven years after opening, this school was one of the highest performing in the state of Indiana, proving that the conservative budgeting approach didn't hamper its academic or creative impact. In fact, just the opposite happened. Once the cash reserve solidified, the school had the financial flexibility to adjust to program needs, expansion, and staffing. Again, school administrators budgeted for less, and ended up with more. That seems counterintuitive at first, but it works.

Use-It-or-Lose-It Spending

As we've described over the previous sections, dynamic yet conservative budgeting is typically most appropriate for smaller schools. The dynamic, conservative budget must have a reserve to protect for risk. Individual schools or small rural districts that allocate every dollar inevitably run out of money. Yes, leaders in these settings need to balance the books, but balancing the books does not imply budgeting every dime until there are all zeros at the bottom. Even small schools that budget for a cash reserve typically have to dip into that reserve by the end of the year. Therefore, it's not a question of whether you should build in extra cash at the end of the year—it's a question of *how much*.

For larger schools or large school systems, things are more static and predictable within the building. If the district or central office's reserve cash (days cash on hand, or DCOH) is low, however, your budget could be tightened, your programming reduced, and pay or hiring freezes initiated. The central office is managing the dynamic flexibility. As a building leader in those larger systems, you'll be operating on a "use it or lose it" model. Your budget is your allocation for the year until you're told otherwise. Whatever you don't use will roll back to the central office. Budgeting down to zero is allowed but is a risky proposition. If you hit zero, there is no harm. If you save the district a few dollars, you look great. Cost the district money, and you're in a bad way. So zero is a nice guidepost, but manage the funds in your control carefully, and understand the realities of your setting.

As you spend down the existing budget or plan for the following year's spending, your effective dollars spent should be reflected in the retention of high-quality staff and school-specific programming. Again, remember your measuring sticks throughout the process, making sure your mission is represented in how your money is spent, and the money spent authentically helps the school.

Rough Calculations

As discussed earlier in this chapter, any school leader should monitor his or her school's budget closely, even if many of the decisions are beyond local control. You are probably not a trained accountant, so the following sections provide guidance for making rough calculations around budgeting and spending. Specifically, we explore measurable budget goals for small schools, predictable income and expenses, and other income and expenses.

Measurable Budget Goals for Small Schools

Remember, in a smaller school setting, you may be assuming the responsibility of managing the entire budget. You'll need some measurables to guide your way. Of course, there are no universal specific financial targets, but there are some basic rules for single sites or small district operations. The appendix (page 184) provides more specific targets, but here are six crucial starting points for your budget process.

1. Underestimate your expected enrollment by 10 percent. For example, if you expect 400 students, budget for no more than 360. This sets up a buffer of income if enrollment comes in as expected.

2. Always know your DCOH (see chapter 1, page 22). Strive to maintain no less than twenty DCOH at the end of the first year, thirty to fifty at the end of the second year, and fifty or more thereafter.

3. Keep salaries and benefits below 85 percent of your total budget. Keep benefits below 30 percent of your total salaries.

4. Allocate less than 5 percent of total income for specific mission and vision creativity. Consider what purchases would advance the school's mission through cultural enhancement, nonacademic programming, fringe benefits, specialized site or grounds enhancements, and so on.

5. Allocate less than 2 percent of total income for building a cash reserve.

6. Keep your school debt or occupancy cost between 15 and 20 percent (see table 8.1). Calculating the gross occupancy percentage requires adding up the operational costs (mortgage, supplies, materials, equipment, rent, professional services, utilities, property tax, and insurance debt payments) and dividing them by the total income (student funding, state and federal grants, and other income). For example, let's say Garilux Elementary School has $1 million per year in occupancy costs and 450 students at $10,000 income per student. Garilux also brings in an additional $1 million in grants and other income for a total of $5.5 million in income. $1 million divided by $5.5 million is 18 percent occupancy cost.

Table 8.1: Debt and Occupancy Cost Guidelines

Debt or Occupancy Cost as a Percentage of Total Income		Result
Extremely High	25 percent	Will force the leader to allocate a smaller portion of the budget to staff salaries and benefits and will limit all creativity.
High	20 percent	A common threshold expectation, but will erode creativity and stifle long-term staff satisfaction and development. Schools in this range should work to decrease this number within three years to keep compounding expenses from impacting staffing.

continued ⇨

Medium	10–15 percent	The sweet spot: This percentage is very manageable with allowance for some growth in creativity and staffing.
Low	5 percent	At 5 percent, schools have site-based flexibility for increasing staffing, adding resources, or adding additional programming.
Extremely Low	0 percent	At 0 percent, your expenses don't exist. While it is uncommon to be in this position, anything below 5 percent will allow the school leader incredible flexibility for staffing and programming.

Predictable Income and Expenses

It doesn't take long to calculate a rough look at the overall budget. To make it work, you'll need to know your per-pupil income or student tuition amount. Multiply that figure by your expected student count and you have generated your basic funding number, or basic income. Basic income estimations like the sample amounts from a fictional school, Railroad Middle School, found in figure 8.2, can allow a new leader to quickly assess expected income. A blank reproducible version of this chart appears in the appendix (page 184).

Railroad Middle School	
Income Source	**Amount**
Enrollment Income	$4,189,352.00
Student Count	651
Per-Pupil Income	$6,435.25
Student Lunch Revenue	$409,486.00
Contribution Income	$27,937.00
Local Grants	$325,500.00
Federal Grants	$368,548.00
Interest Income	$1,200.00
Other Income	$210,460.00
Total Income	**$5,532,483.25**

Figure 8.2: School income.

Different types of schools will have different sources of income. For example, private schools will see a much larger contribution income line, and traditional public schools will have very little (if any) in that line. Regardless, this "napkin math" method of income analysis is fast and informative. Next, you need to understand expenses. Even if you don't know the exact totals for each category of expenses, you'll have access to enough information—or to board members, central office staff, or bookkeepers who can get it for you—to create a snapshot look at expenses. Figure 8.3 shows the expenses side of Railroad Middle School's balance sheet. It shows an example in action, and the appendix (page 185) includes a blank reproducible version.

Railroad Middle School	
Expense	**Amount**
Total Salaries and Benefits	$3,077,027
Mortgage or Rent Payable	$352,776
Supplies, Materials, and Equipment	$82,350
Other Physical Improvements	$214,420
Professional Services and Subcontracts	$152,410
Utilities and Property Taxes	$115,877
Insurance	$36,350
Other Expenses (Nonacademic programming, fringe benefits, site enhancements, nonessential staffing, and so on)	$210,460
Total Expense	**$4,241,670**

Figure 8.3: School expenses.

Other Income and Expenses

Schools tend to distinguish themselves in the "other income" category. In all classes of schools, this is the income stream designated specifically for your site and the ongoing work there. Often, this income derives from restricted local grants or restricted donations. Restricted funds are earmarked for an identified use and must be spent in that manner. Other funds can also come in the form of discretionary cash, which usually carries fewer stipulations. This cash is typically smaller grant dollars given to the school for general use, allowing the school to spend it at its own discretion. School leaders receiving discretionary funding often have site-based flexibility on expenses such as stipends, bonuses, equipment, curriculum, and so on. Whether restricted or unrestricted, the use of income from the "other" category is where a school leader can be creative. These funds allow you to apply your own spin to the school. A very flexible system would have 5 to 8 percent of the total budget available. The sample budget for Railroad Middle School in figure 8.2 (page 160) has a decent 3.8 percent. More rigid systems allow less than 1 percent. If you're in a setting with a fair amount of local budgeting control, reserving or preallocating funds for creativity will allow for additional flexibility throughout the budget year. It is a great day when this funding can be used to stipend creative efforts, afford an additional staff member, start a mission-oriented club, fund a series of parent events, and so on. This kind of flexibility can make a solid impact on the culture and energy driving your day-to-day process.

> **Pause & Reflect**
>
> Can you leverage your existing budget to find pitfalls in your school's spending plan?
>
> Have you defined which funds within your budget are yours to allocate?
>
> Have you calculated your true costs? Account for occupancy, staffing, creativity, per-pupil income, daily cost of operation, and so on.

Federal Grants

When considering federal funding for education, note that the United States has specific programs designed for supporting education. Many of these programs funnel funding through states down to the local level. In other countries, the process is similar. In Australia, for example, the government supplements the states and territories with additional educational funding for governmental schools but provides a majority of funding for nongovernmental schools. In Canada, funding control for education is more tightly controlled at the provincial level. For the purposes of this discussion, we will continue with a context of U.S. government funding.

When reviewing income, new leaders need to be aware of the competitive and noncompetitive funding streams from the federal government. For most schools in the United States, funding is available through the Elementary and Secondary Education Act (ESEA) depending on the socioeconomic and demographic population of the school. This funding is often referred to as *title funding*. Under ESEA, there are specific programs designed to provide additional funding for particular educational purposes. Title I, Improving the Academic Achievement of the Disadvantaged, and Title II, Preparing, Training, and Recruiting High Quality Teachers and Principals, are two common examples. Larger school systems will typically handle all ESEA funding for their schools at the district or corporation level and allow that funding to filter downstream in the form of supports and equipment. Conversely, many private schools opt out of federal funding to remain autonomous, since federal funds come with federal oversight. Still, a majority of U.S. schools typically opt into federal funding; for schools in underprivileged areas of the country, securing these funds can be critical to the success of the school.

To provide a launching point for exploration and comparison, the appendix (page 186) provides a list of many of the federal funds available in the United States. After reviewing federal programming, it's important to assess whether the grant requirements for the funding can add value to the mission and vision of the school. In larger public settings, these vetting decisions are made for you by the central office, but proper grant implementation is still under your authority. If the implementation, reporting, and partnership requirements overtax your model, the federal program may weaken your system. If the grant is aligned to your model, your school is more likely to truly benefit from the funding.

As an example, let's assume you've qualified for Title I, Part A funding. This grant is designed to improve academic outcomes for disadvantaged students. Figures 8.4 and 8.5 (page 164) represent a typical allocation in a fictional urban school, along with a typical budget for that same allocation. The appendix (page 187) contains a template you can use for Title I budget allocations.

While every organization prioritizes funding differently, note the amount of income in the Title I budget spent outside of academic instruction in figure 8.5. The school has allocated $50,000 to operations and maintenance, among other nonacademic distributions. This income distribution points out a common flaw in how schools utilize federal funding sources. While it's important to leverage funding to strengthen the supplemental programming allowed by Title I, Part A, this budget appears to allocate less than half of the award to the educational process. While a $340,000 award sounds like an attractive amount, schools with this budget could feel burdened by the processes of monitoring the appropriate application of the grant along seven categories, and then coordinating those expenses as they purchase things that may or may not enhance student learning. Therein lies the trap. As you

District and School Name	TriCity Schools—Aleen Elementary
Program Type	Targeted Assistance School (TAS) or Schoolwide Programs (SWP)
School's Allocation	$340,000

Figure 8.4: Title I award.

Instruction	$60,000
Instructional Support	$80,000
Improvement	$80,000
Other Support Services	$45,000
Refund of Revenue	$0
Operations and Maintenance	$50,000
Transportation	$10,000
Community Service	$15,000

Figure 8.5: Title I budget allocations.

contemplate the benefits and challenges of federal funding, use the blank reproducible template provided in the appendix (page 187) as a basis for your own allocations.

Federal awards are complex, but the complexities are more tolerable if the funds help offset costs that directly align with your mission and vision. Any time you can supplement, not supplant, the budget for your model of instruction, then staffing, equipment, or services funded by federal dollars will feel like a financial win. But if you use federal money in ways that do not directly contribute to your school's core goals, then the money becomes a burden, even a potential hurdle to student growth, because of the complications of unnecessary purchases and management of funding. Every dollar in a federal grant must be tracked and reported, which is a significant task for smaller school districts or single-site schools. Making that more challenging is the fact that most federal grants are *reimbursable grants*, meaning you only receive the grant after you spend your allocation. Then, you (or your district) submit a reimbursement to the managing agency and the money you spent is released.

After reading this, you may be thinking, Why would anyone want federal funding? The answer to that question takes us back once again to our concept of a laser focus on strategic systems and the utilization of measuring sticks. Federal funding can be an amazing tool for advancing your mission and vision and authentically improving your school. And, these grants typically come in six-figure allocations, so they're hard to ignore. The key is to stay strategic and to align available grant funds with the task of improving your operation. These dollars can have a considerable impact but need to be used purposefully to move the school system forward.

Other Sources of Supplemental Funding

In general, schools leverage student-based funding (tuition dollars or per-pupil enrollment funds) as the most consistent source of income for maintaining their annual budget. But, additional cash helps sustain the forward momentum of the institution. As we've explained, access to federal or other governmental funding can help expand the budget. However, federal funding may not be readily available for private schools and may not be enough to supplement the traditional public or charter sector. So, how do we find the money to sustain our programming?

To begin with, let's go back to the concept of DCOH (days cash on hand; see chapter 1, page 22). Basically, DCOH is your cash reserve. We recommended more than fifty DCOH as a stable cash reserve, with eighty or more marking a very healthy reserve. At the district or township level, cash reserves are handled by the central office and typically carry much stronger DCOH figures than individual charter or private schools. Because they are much smaller organizations, it's important for the charter and private sectors to protect themselves with reserve funding. The simplest way to achieve this is conservative budgeting, as mentioned earlier in this chapter. In other words, plan for lower enrollment and higher costs. In this way, you've budgeted for catastrophe and, when the year averages out, you'll typically realize a fair amount of savings. Budgeting conservatively does produce savings, but it's very tempting to spend those savings as the year progresses, which will negate gains and leave you right back where you started, so be careful in this approach.

In the traditional public sector, excess cash is typically funneled back to the central office for the main district, township, or province. These reserves help replenish the ongoing operating capital of the larger educational organization, but do not directly impact the individual school (aside from making the school leader look like a great manager of money). However, regardless of the school type, a large cash reserve or savings coupled with low student performance can appear to be a reflection of poor leadership. In these cases, the process of building cash reserves needs to be very clearly articulated with buy-in at every administrative level.

While conservative budgeting is an effective tool for developing additional cash, another great way to build additional income is to simply build enrollment. Additional cash may be hard to find; enrollment is the most dependable source of income. Thus, enrollment marketing, no matter the setting, is a key component of the budgetary process. In their book, *Marketing Management for School Leaders*, Deidre Pettinga, Azure Angelov, and David Bateman (2019) explain it this way:

> School leaders as marketing experts is a new phenomenon created by the advent of school choice. Schools are operating in an environment of unprecedented options for parents to choose from, including traditional public schools, private schools, voucher schools, charter schools, and homeschooling. (p. 16)

Put simply, marketing the school helps to fill seats. Full seats protect the budget and provide additional revenue. Marketing should be a well-honed tool in a school leader's toolbox, but it should be used strategically and with measuring sticks. In other words, don't jeopardize your mission and vision just to fill seats. Enrollment gimmicks, giveaways, and lofty promises may yield early enrollment interest, but those same efforts could destabilize a school culture you've worked very hard to establish. Instead, getting the word out about your academic successes, student and staff stories, facilities, programming, accomplishments, and so on will help draw the most sustainable interest.

The key to your marketing efforts is to invest in your school's identity. Whether large or small, every school has a particular identity that can set it apart from others. This identity is a key differentiator. Even though it can seem like all schools in a district are cut from the same cloth, when you look deeper into culture, operations, growth, staffing, and communications, individual differences become more obvious. Consider this quote from *Urban Education* (DiMartino & Jessen, 2016):

> The branding decisions a school makes—from the name, to the official theme, to decisions about gender enrollment—affect how parents and prospective students perceive the school and, in turn, who decides to enroll. At the same time, schools with a low marketing profile can be passed over by students, simply due to lack of familiarity. (p. 448)

As a leader, you'll be tasked with marketing decisions that have the potential to elevate your program and make it the best option for those with access to it. When you find that authentic, mission-related differentiator that generates enrollment interest, don't hesitate to raise its prominence in your marketing approach.

Once you've honed your school identity, consider your digital marketing approach. There are many companies with digital marketing savvy who can design an approach for your school including social media, web content, and news media. While this may not have been part of a school's budgeting process in prior decades, money spent on marketing may well pay itself back with enrollment increases. Additionally, when marketed well, a school's local presence is more accessible to the greater community. This can build awareness and lead to additional interest and funding opportunities from philanthropists and corporate donors.

Summary

Finances and budgeting can be an intimidating topic not only for new leaders but also for experienced leaders in new settings. The amount of control you have over your school's budget will vary depending on school type and local circumstances. Regardless of your specific situation, it's important to understand your budget boundaries, take an appropriate approach to planning and spending, and do some rough calculations to stay informed and prepared in this essential area. We also touched on federal grants and the benefits and challenges that come along with this funding source. Remember that marketing and identity should be a part of your budget considerations, and that strong enrollment is the most stabilizing factor in your school's budget.

Chapter 8 Reflection Questions

1. For your specific school setting, what portion of the school's finances do you control? Reflect on which areas you control and which of those have the highest impact on school outcomes.

2. What are the similarities and differences between dynamic budgeting and conservative budgeting?

3. What measurable budget goals do you need to set in the coming year based on your school's needs?

4. How will you use any remaining discretionary funding to increase creativity or boost the mission-specific identity of your school?

5. Which federal funding sources are best aligned to your school? How can they be leveraged to add value to the mission and vision?

Epilogue

Your first year as the principal of a school will be a rewarding challenge. Whether you are a first-time principal, an experienced leader taking a new position, or a pioneer opening a brand-new school, we hope this book provides useful guidance for tackling the realities of educational leadership. To be sure, your new culture will throw a variety of problems your way. Things that you think will surely work will backfire, and things you think are destined for failure will mysteriously succeed. Staff hires that seem sure bets will flounder, and superstars will emerge from unexpected places. Stay flexible and learn from every unforeseen result. Accept the surprise wins and be willing to scrap ideas that consume your resources without producing results.

As you respond to new challenges, remember that countless educators have taken on the task of school leadership before you. Learn from them. Ask your colleagues and mentors for guidance. Borrow every great theory, idea, philosophy, model, curricular tool, and evaluation process you can get your hands on. Whenever you can simplify your task by standing on the shoulders of others, take advantage. Doing extra work just to prove you can do extra work might feel good, but it will likely come at the expense of something else that needs your time.

Define your priorities and stay focused on the essential elements we've discussed throughout this book: your mission and vision, strategic systems, relationships, staff development, academic models, and effective delegation. Put yourself in a proactive position for success by creating strong systems before the first day of school. Focus on the long game when developing your outcomes with staff and students. Stay objective and make sure decisions are based on data and growth. Balance your approach to maintain buy-in from your staff. Lastly, remember norms and how important they are for growing a strong, stable culture.

School leadership is a very hard job, and not to be taken lightly. There's no college course or graduate school program that can fully prepare leaders for the realities of a new school setting. It's not the kind of job where one climbs up the rungs just to sit back and enjoy being the boss. This job must be grounded in an honest passion, because without that passion, you'll never survive the challenges and hard work. In terms of impact, being a school leader is one of the greatest jobs in the world. Over the course of a career, a school leader may affect hundreds of teachers and thousands of students. Done right, the cumulative effect of successful leadership on staff and students can spark real, positive change in our global society. As you begin this school leadership journey, keep that aspiration in mind and heart. The world needs you!

APPENDIX

Reproducibles

The reproducibles in this appendix are designed to help school leaders enact the recommendations in this book.

- "Initial Walkthrough Checklist" (page 172)
- "Basic Budget Considerations" (page 175)
- "Beginning-of-the-Year Preparations Checklist" (page 177)
- "Facility Checklist" (page 178)
- "Vendor and Subcontractor Contact List" (page 181)
- "Budget Contact List" (page 183)
- "School Income Template" (page 184)
- "School Expenses Template" (page 185)
- "Federal Funding Programs" (page 186)
- "Title I Budget Template" (page 187)

Visit **go.SolutionTree.com/leadership** to download each one.

Initial Walkthrough Checklist

1. Is the building secured by an electronic security system or by physical keys?
   - ☐ If electronic: Does the system work? Who provides service?
   - ☐ If keyed: Who is the key master? Where is key storage?

2. What kind of system heats, cools, and regulates air quality in the building?
   - ☐ Who manages the heating, ventilation, and air-conditioning?
   - ☐ Who manages air quality regulations for the building?

3. What are the building's faults? Check for the following.
   - ☐ Broken or jammed windows
   - ☐ Blocked exits
   - ☐ Mold
   - ☐ Evidence of roof or wall leaks on ceiling tiles, staircases, walls, and flooring
   - ☐ Evidence of basement or ground-level flooding
   - ☐ Rodent or other pest issues
   - ☐ Lack of air-conditioning
   - ☐ Aging heating systems
   - ☐ Aging boiler system
   - ☐ Faulty security
   - ☐ Inadequate or inoperative lighting
   - ☐ Inoperable restrooms or water fountains

4. Is there a whole-school intercom or other communication system?
   - ☐ Is it functional?
   - ☐ Are there phones in all rooms?

5. What are the hallway conditions?
   - ☐ How wide are they? If the halls are narrow, additional procedures will be needed to manage traffic.
   - ☐ Do the building materials of the halls amplify or dampen sound? The more echo or reverberation, the more that needs to be done to de-stress that environment.

6. What is the classroom configuration?
   - ☐ Are there enough classrooms for anticipated classes? If not, how was this handled the previous year?

- ☐ Is there ample teaching space? Counting ceiling tiles can help you quickly measure classroom size. Most ceiling tiles are two-by-four-foot rectangles. A thirty-by-thirty-foot space is an optimal size for twenty-five to thirty students.

7. What is the building's layout?
   - ☐ If there are multiple floors or wings utilized by students and staff, walk them all. Take the time to get a feel for regular routes through the school.
   - ☐ What are the sightlines and blind spots?
   - ☐ Check other areas.
     - ☐ Inspect all closets and alcoves.
     - ☐ Inspect restrooms. See how they're laid out. Test flush a few toilets.
     - ☐ Check faucets and fountains.
     - ☐ Locate all utility panels. Find out where the master breaker is.
     - ☐ Check every fire extinguisher to see when it was last inspected.
     - ☐ Walk through the kitchen. Is it clean? Does it appear operable?
     - ☐ Check the gym. Are there bleachers? Do they open? Is there a stage? Do the lights and PA system work?
   - ☐ If there are any unused spaces (basement, crawlspace, attic), have a look. You need to know your building from top to bottom.
   - ☐ Find the roof access and walk the roof. Check for obvious problems and give the property and surrounding neighborhood a good look.
   - ☐ A working elevator is required for all multifloor buildings. Check that yours has had its annual inspection.
   - ☐ Check overall building accessibility, ramps, wheelchair-accessible restrooms, and so on.

8. Lastly, is the building secure?
   - ☐ Is the front office secure?
   - ☐ Are all entrances to the facility secure?
   - ☐ Where are the overall vulnerabilities?
   - ☐ What more will need to be done when determining fire routes, lockdowns, crisis and evacuation plans, and so on?

After completing the walkthrough, schedule a meeting with building janitorial or physical plant operations to review your notes and get a feel for what can or can't be done to address any problems you've found.

In charter or private schools, meet with the board members or executive director to discuss your findings and glean which of your concerns they are already aware of, and whether other concerns may need to be elevated in priority.

Next, meet with your administrative team to go over your concerns surrounding building functionality (hallway size, classroom size, noise, traffic patterns, and so on). Explore past solutions and begin to delegate the design of new solutions as needed.

Remember, the goal of the walkthrough is to understand the facility. There will always be issues that can't readily be solved, but no issue can be solved until it's discovered.

Basic Budget Considerations

Expense	Percentage of Ongoing Income Streams
Salaries and benefits	70–85 percent
Occupancy (debt payments, supplies, utilities, technology, operations, and so on)	10–15 percent
Creativity (site-based individuality)	Remainder

Debt or Occupancy Cost as a Percentage of Total Income		Result
Extremely High	25 percent	Will force the leader to allocate a smaller portion of the budget to staff salaries and benefits and will limit all creativity.
High	20 percent	A common threshold expectation, but will erode creativity and stifle long-term staff satisfaction and development. Schools in this range should work to decrease this number within three years to avoid compounding expenses from impacting staffing.
Medium	10–15 percent	The sweet spot: This percentage is very manageable with allowance for some growth in creativity and staffing.
Low	5 percent	At 5 percent, schools have site-based flexibility for increasing staffing, adding resources, or adding additional programming.
Extremely Low	0 percent	At 0 percent, your expenses don't exist. While it is uncommon to be in this position, anything below 5 percent will allow the school leader incredible flexibility for staffing and programming.

How to Find the Money	Details
Build a cash reserve.	Budget low: use a conservative budget plan.
Sell your model.	Market safely: don't create an identity that can't be funded.
Invest in identity.	Focus on your mission: don't sacrifice your model for funding.

Budgeting 101	Actions
Follow percentage guides.	Utilize the budget like a data tool, impersonally and nonemotionally.
Create minimum cash reserves.	Fifty or more days cash on hand is a good goal. Divide ongoing annual expenses by 365 to determine daily cost of operation and strive to save more than fifty times that amount.
Resist urgency.	Stay conservative—never reach for a deal.
Lower the debt.	Whenever possible, the first option should be to pay off debt.
Beat your budget.	Budget conservatively, especially on enrollment and nonguaranteed income. Leave a cushion in the annual budget for unexpected expenses.

Beginning-of-the-Year Preparations Checklist

The following checklists are designed as a starting point for opening preparations and school operations. These lists can be a valuable guide for customizing your school's functionality.

Preparing Staff

- ❒ Develop schoolwide and classroom procedures and systems.
- ❒ Complete faculty handbook.
- ❒ Plan and schedule professional development and teacher report days.
- ❒ Send welcome letter to faculty and staff.
- ❒ Complete any remaining hiring.
- ❒ Hold opening faculty meeting.

Preparing the Logistics

- ❒ Devise master schedule.
- ❒ Complete master calendar.
- ❒ Oversee classroom setup.
- ❒ Determine bus schedule.
- ❒ Engineer parking and traffic flow.
- ❒ Determine bell schedule.
- ❒ Schedule locker combination rollover.
- ❒ Perform summer deep cleaning.
- ❒ Communicate logistics to other departments.

Preparing Families

- ❒ Send out back-to-school packets and summer mailings.
- ❒ Plan and schedule registration and meet-the-teacher events.
- ❒ Generate automated information calls and send emails to families.

Preparing for Special Populations

- ❒ Acquire and read legal guidebooks (*Wrightslaw: Special Education Law* and your state or province's special education law).
- ❒ Obtain contact information for your special education counsel.
- ❒ Prepare an equity statement for the school.
- ❒ Ensure the school is physically accessible to all.

Lead From the Start © 2020 Solution Tree Press • SolutionTree.com
Visit **go.SolutionTree.com/leadership** to download this free reproducible.

Facility Checklist

Maintaining a facility is an arduous task, and not one to be taken lightly. When the facility breaks down, the leader is the first line of defense. Understanding the physical plant and how the building functions is critically important. The following checklists will help new leaders conduct thorough walkthroughs of their property.

Maintenance

Plumbing

- ☐ Check all faucets.
- ☐ Check all toilets.
- ☐ Check all water fountains.
- ☐ Check all kitchen plumbing.
- ☐ Check all outside hose spigots.

Electrical

- ☐ Test all outlets.
- ☐ Inspect all breaker boxes.
- ☐ Check all interior lights.
- ☐ Check all exterior lights.
- ☐ Check for code compliance for power in classrooms and offices.
- ☐ Check exterior outlets.
- ☐ Check exterior power lines running into the building.

Heating, Ventilation, and Air-Conditioning (HVAC)

- ☐ Understand where the HVAC units are in your building.
- ☐ Determine who will have roof and HVAC access.
- ☐ Have the HVAC service provider conduct a walkthrough of the entire HVAC system including building zones and thermostats.

Code Enforcement

- ☐ Check for high weeds and grass.
- ☐ Check for poorly lit or faulty signage.
- ☐ Check for exposed wiring or damaged fencing.
- ☐ Check trees for threatening limbs.

Landscaping

- ☐ Determine timing for mowing and trimming the landscape.
- ☐ Determine responsibility for flowerbed maintenance and shrub and tree trimming.
- ☐ Determine the depth threshold for snow removal and ice salting.

Bad Weather Closure Plan

- ☐ Contact local media to determine how to broadcast school closures and delays.
- ☐ Test the school's parent-notification system.
- ☐ Review the school's emergency phone trees or communication plans.

Building Security

- ☐ Test the school's security system.
- ☐ Determine all access codes and levels of access for the security system.
- ☐ Work with local law enforcement or school resource officer team to plan all emergency preparedness drills.
- ☐ Determine an alternate evacuation site should the building become inhabitable.

Other Services

Technology

- ☐ Refresh all end-user devices.
- ☐ Check for connectivity through all wireless access points.
- ☐ Check server speed and firewall integrity.
- ☐ Reset site Wi-Fi passwords.
- ☐ Check life span of local server.
- ☐ Check server room cleanliness, cabling, and connectivity.

Food Service

- ☐ Ensure that the kitchen looks clean, such that one would feel comfortable serving or eating food prepared on the surfaces.
- ☐ Ensure that the dry food is stored off the floor and in a separate area.
- ☐ Ensure that the food in the cold storage is dated and labeled.
- ☐ Ensure that there is ample room for washing dishes, with a hand-washing area separate from the dishwashing area.
- ☐ Ensure all faucets work.
- ☐ Ensure all the equipment powers on.

- ☐ Ensure that the freezers have working temperature gauges, and that they are below zero degrees Fahrenheit.
- ☐ Ensure that the refrigerators have working temperature gauges, and that they are above freezing but below forty degrees.
- ☐ Ensure that the ceiling vents and stove vent hoods are clean.
- ☐ Ensure that the walls are a single light color with a cleanable surface.
- ☐ Ensure that there is a cleaning schedule for the area.
- ☐ Ensure that the food warmers have a temperature sensor, or that they are tracked for temperature throughout food service.

Lead From the Start © 2020 Solution Tree Press • SolutionTree.com
Visit **go.SolutionTree.com/leadership** to download this free reproducible.

Vendor and Subcontractor Contact List

Plumbing	Name:	
	Phone:	Email:
Electrical	Name:	
	Phone:	Email:
HVAC	Name:	
	Phone:	Email:
Exterminator	Name:	
	Phone:	Email:
Landscaping	Name:	
	Phone:	Email:
Building security	Name:	
	Phone:	Email:
Local code enforcement	Name:	
	Phone:	Email:
Bad weather closure	Name:	
	Phone:	Email:
Technology	Name:	
	Phone:	Email:
Food service	Name:	
	Phone:	Email:
Playground inspection	Name:	
	Phone:	Email:

page 1 of 2

Transportation	Name:	
	Phone:	Email:
Counseling	Name:	
	Phone:	Email:
Accounting	Name:	
	Phone:	Email:
Human resources	Name:	
	Phone:	Email:
Legal counsel	Name:	
	Phone:	Email:

Budget Contact List

Federal grants manager	Name:	
	Phone:	Email:
State (provincial) department of education	Name:	
	Phone:	Email:
District budget manager	Name:	
	Phone:	Email:
Bank	Name:	
	Phone:	Email:
Debt holders	Name:	
	Phone:	Email:
Accounting firm	Name:	
	Phone:	Email:
Insurance providers	Name:	
	Phone:	Email:
Staffing coordinator	Name:	
	Phone:	Email:
Curriculum vendors	Name:	
	Phone:	Email:

School Income Template

Income Source	Amount
Enrollment Income	
Student Count	
Per-Pupil Income	
Student Lunch Revenue	
Contribution Income	
Local Grants	
Federal Grants	
Interest Income	
Other Income	
Total Income	

School Expenses Template

Expense	Amount
Total Salaries and Benefits	
Mortgage or Rent Payable	
Supplies, Materials, and Equipment	
Other Physical Improvements	
Professional Services and Subcontracts	
Utilities and Property Taxes	
Insurance	
Other Expenses	
Total Expense	

Federal Funding Programs

The following list includes many of the funds available from the U.S. government. A quick online search of each program will help new leaders understand what kinds of federal funding may be suitable for their schools.

- Improving the Academic Achievement of the Disadvantaged, Title I, Part A
- School Improvement Grants, Title I, Part A, Section 1003(g)
- Migrant Education Program, Title I, Part C
- Neglected, Delinquent, and At-Risk Youth, Title I, Part D
- Dropout Prevention Act, Title I, Part H
- Teacher and Principal Training and Recruiting Fund, Title II, Part A
- Language Instruction for Limited English Proficient and Immigrant Students, Title III
- Safe and Drug-Free Schools and Communities Act, Title IV, Part A
- 21st Century Community Learning Centers, Title IV, Part B
- Promise Neighborhoods/Fund for the Improvement of Education, Title V, Part D
- Elementary and Secondary School Counseling Program, Title V, Part D
- Rural Education Initiative, Title VI, Part B, Subparts 1 and 2
- Indian Education Formula Grants, Title VII, Part A, Subpart 1
- McKinney-Vento Homeless Education Assistance Improvements Act of 2001, Subtitle B of Title VII of McKinney-Vento Homeless Assistance Act
- Indian Education Special Programs and Projects to Improve Educational Opportunities for Indian Children, Title VII, Part A, Subpart 2
- Alaska Native Education, Title VII, Part C

Title I Budget Template

School Name	
Program Type	Targeted Assistance School (TAS) or Schoolwide Programs (SWP)
School's Allocation	
Instruction	
Support	
Improvement	
Other Support Services	
Refund of Revenue	
Operations and Maintenance	
Transportation	
Community Service	

Lead From the Start © 2020 Solution Tree Press • SolutionTree.com
Visit **go.SolutionTree.com/leadership** to download this free reproducible.

References and Resources

Ainsworth, L. (2003). *Power standards: Identifying the standards that matter the most.* Englewood, CO: Advanced Learning Press.

Ainsworth, L. (2013). *Prioritizing the Common Core: Identifying specific standards to emphasize the most.* Englewood, CO: Lead + Learn Press.

Akhtari, M., Moreira, D., & Trucco, L. (2017). Political turnover, bureaucratic turnover, and the quality of public services. *SSRN.* Accessed at https://ssrn.com/abstract=2538354 on September 6, 2019.

American Bar Association. (2016). *School-to-prison pipeline.* Accessed at https://www.americanbar.org/groups/child_law/resources/attorneys/school-to-prison-pipeline/ on May 31, 2019.

Australian Curriculum, Assessment and Reporting Authority (ACARA). (2019). *National Report on Schooling in Australia 2017.* Accessed at https://www.acara.edu.au/docs/default-source/default-document-library/national-report-on-schooling-in-australia-20170de312404c94637ead88ff00003e0139.pdf?sfvrsn=0 on September 6, 2019.

Bambrick-Santoyo, P. (2018). *Leverage leadership 2.0: A practical guide to building exceptional schools.* San Francisco: Jossey-Bass.

Bartanen, B., Grissom, J., & Rogers, L. (2019). The impacts of principal turnover. *Educational Evaluation and Policy Analysis, 41*(3), 350–374.

Bartoletti, J., & Connelly, G. (2013). *Leadership matters: What the research says about the importance of principal leadership.* Accessed at http://www.naesp.org/sites/default/files/LeadershipMatters.pdf on June 9, 2019.

Beam, A., Claxton, R. L., & Smith, S. J. (2016). Challenges for novice school leaders: Facing today's issues in school administration. *Scholars Crossing.* Accessed at http://digitalcommons.liberty.edu/educ_fac_pubs/233 on June 21, 2019.

Bluyssen, P. (2017). Health, comfort and performance of children in classrooms—New directions for research. *Indoor and Built Environment, 26*(8), 1040–1050.

Bowd, J., Bowles, T., & McKenzie, V. (2016). An exploratory analysis of the personal, school and demographic variables affecting the homework effort of Australian secondary students. Paper presented at *Australian Association for Research in Education* Conference, Melbourne.

Brieant, A., Holmes, C. J., Deater-Deckard, K., King-Casas, B., & Kim-Spoon, J. (2017). Household chaos as a context for intergenerational transmission of executive functioning. *Journal of Adolescence, 58,* 40–48.

Buckingham, M. (2005). *The one thing you need to know: About great managing, great leading, and sustained individual success.* New York: Free Press.

Buffum, A. G., Mattos, M. W., & Malone, J. (2018). *Taking action: A handbook for RTI at Work.* Bloomington, IN: Solution Tree Press.

Cheryan, S., Ziegler, S. A., Plaut, V. C., & Meltzoff, A. N. (2014). Designing classrooms to maximize student achievement. *Policy Insights From the Behavioral and Brain Sciences, 1*(1), 4–12.

Coalition for Juvenile Justice. (2019). *Recommendations to the 116th Congress.* Accessed at http://www.juvjustice.org/sites/default/files/resource-files/Recommendationsforthe%20 116th.pdf on May 31, 2019.

Collins, J. (2005). *Good to great and the social sectors: A monograph to accompany* Good to great: Why some companies make the leap—and others don't. Boulder, CO: Author.

Corbett, M. (2015). From law to folklore: Work stress and the Yerkes-Dodson law. *Journal of Managerial Psychology, 30*(6), 741–752.

Cornman, S. Q., Zhou, L., Howell, M. R., & Young, J. (2018). *Revenues and expenditures for public elementary and secondary education: School year 2014–15 (fiscal year 2015): First look* (NCES 2018–301). Washington, DC: National Center for Education Statistics.

Darling, N. (2011). Why threats don't work: Parenting effectively. *Psychology Today.* Accessed at https://www.psychologytoday.com/us/blog/thinking-about-kids/201101/why-threats -dont-work-parenting-effectively on August 13, 2019.

Decker, J. (2014). Legal literacy in education: An ideal time to increase research, advocacy, and action. *Education Law Reporter, 304*(1), 679–696.

Dede, C. (2010). Reflection on the draft national education technology plan 2010: Foundations for transformation. *Educational Technology, 50*(6), 18–22.

De Jong, D., Grundmeyer, T., & Yankey, J. (2017). Identifying and addressing themes of job dissatisfaction for secondary principals. *School Leadership & Management, 37*(4), 354–371.

Democracy Collaborative. (n.d.). Anchor institutions. *Community-Wealth.* Accessed at https:// community-wealth.org/strategies/panel/anchors/index.html on November 17, 2018.

Dhuey, E., & Smith, J. (2017). How school principals influence student learning. *Empirical Economics, 54*(2), 851–882.

DiMartino, C., & Jessen, S. (2016). School brand management. *Urban Education, 51*(5), 447–475.

Dunbar, R. I. (2016). Do online social media cut through the constraints that limit the size of offline social networks? *Royal Society Open Science*, *3*(1), 150292.

EdTech Strategies. (2015). *Pencils down: The shift to online & computer-based testing*. Accessed at https://www.edtechstrategies.com/wp-content/uploads/2015/11/PencilsDownK-8_EdTech-StrategiesLLC.pdf on September 6, 2019.

Emotional intelligence. (2019). In *Lexico*. Accessed at https://www.lexico.com/en/definition/emotional_intelligence on September 6, 2019.

Fay, J., & Fay, C. (2012). *Parenting the love and logic way*. Golden, CO: The Love and Logic Institute.

Fortner, K., Normore, A. H., & Brooks, J. S. (2019). Digital equity and its role in the digital divide. In A. H. Normore & A. I. Lahera (Eds.), *Crossing the bridge of the digital divide: A walk with global leaders* (pp. 3–18). Charlotte, NC: Information Age Publishing.

Garcia, S., & Cottrell, D. (2002). *Listen up, teacher! You are making a difference!* Horseshoe Bay, TX: Cornerstone Leadership Institute.

Gardner, D. (2009). *The science of fear: How the culture of fear manipulates your brain*. New York: Plume.

Gardner, L. Y. (2016). *Principals' perceptions about the elements of mentoring that most support the development of a new principal's leadership capacity* Doctoral dissertation. Accessed at http://hdl.handle.net/10342/5383 on June 9, 2019.

Gladwell, M. (2002). *The tipping point: How little things can make a big difference*. Boston: Back Bay Books.

Goleman, D. (2004, January). What makes a leader? *Harvard Business Review*. Accessed at https://hbr.org/2004/01/what-makes-a-leader on September 6, 2019.

Goodman, J. F., & Cook, B. I. (2019). Shaming school children: A violation of fundamental rights? *Theory and Research in Education*, *17*(1), 62–81.

Haft, S., Witt, P. J., Thomas, T. (Producers), & Weir, P. (Director). (1989). *Dead poets society* [Motion picture]. United States: Touchstone Pictures.

Harlacher, J. E. (2015). *Designing effective classroom management*. Bloomington, IN: Marzano Resources.

Harlacher, J. E., & Rodriguez, B. J. (2017). *An educator's guide to schoolwide positive behavioral interventions and supports*. Bloomington, IN: Marzano Resources.

Henderson, A. T. (2007). *Beyond the bake sale: The essential guide to family-school partnerships*. New York: New Press.

Hewitt, C. D. (2017). *An analytic synthesis of research studies dealing with the relationship between school building condition and student academic achievement*. Unpublished doctoral dissertation, Virginia Polytechnic Institute and State University, Blacksburg.

Horng, E. L., Klasik, D., & Loeb, S. (2010). Principal's time use and school effectiveness. *American Journal of Education, 116*(4), 491–523.

Jackson, D. (2017). Integrated multi-tiered systems of support: Blending RTI and PBIS. *Perspectives on Language and Literacy, 43*(3), 49–50.

Jacob, H., Kreifelts, B., Nizielski, S., Schütz, A., & Wildgruber, D. (2016). Effects of emotional intelligence on the impression of irony created by the mismatch between verbal and nonverbal cues. *PLOS One*. Accessed at https://journals.plos.org/plosone/article?id=10.1371/journal.pone.0163211 on July 3, 2019.

Keating, K., Rosch, D., & Burgoon, L. (2014). Developmental readiness for leadership: The differential effects of leadership courses on creating "ready, willing, and able" leaders. *Journal of Leadership Education, 13*(3), 1–16.

Kurtz, G. (Producer), & Lucas, G. (Director). (1977). *Star wars: Episode IV—A new hope* [Motion picture]. United States: 20th Century Fox.

Lee, C., & Fernandez, M. A. (2017). Emotional encoding context leads to memory bias in individuals with high anxiety. *Brain Sciences*. Accessed at https://doi.org/10.3390/brainsci8010006 on July 3, 2019.

Lemov, D. (2015). *Teach like a champion 2.0: 62 techniques that put students on the path to college*. San Francisco: Jossey-Bass.

Louis, K. S., Leithwood, K., Wahlstrom, K. L., & Anderson, S. E. (2010). *Investigating the links to improved student learning: Final report of research findings*. Accessed at https://www.wallacefoundation.org/knowledge-center/Documents/Investigating-the-Links-to-Improved-Student-Learning.pdf on May 15, 2019.

Loveless, T. (2014). *The 2014 Brown Center report on American education: How well are American students learning?* Accessed at https://www.brookings.edu/research/homework-in-america/ on December 11, 2018.

MacNeil, A. J., Prater, D. L., & Busch, S. (2009). The effects of school culture and climate on student achievement. *International Journal of Leadership in Education, 12*(1), 73–84.

Marzano, R. J., Norford, J. S., & Ruyle, M. (2019). *The new art and science of classroom assessment*. Bloomington, IN: Solution Tree.

Marzano, R. J., Warrick, P. B., & Simms, J. A. (2014). *A handbook for high reliability schools: The next step in school reform*. Bloomington, IN: Marzano Resources.

Mayworm, A., & Sharkey, J. (2014). Ethical considerations in a three-tiered approach to school discipline policy and practice. *Psychology in the Schools, 51*(7), 693–704.

McAdams, R. (1997). A systems approach to school reform. *Phi Delta Kappan, 79*(2), 138–143.

Metzger, M. W., Fowler, P. J., & Swanstrom, T. (2018). Hypermobility and educational outcomes: The case of St. Louis. *Urban Education, 53*(6), 774–805.

Muhammad, A. (2009, February). *Transforming school culture: Eliminating staff division to improve student performance*. Presentation at Professional Learning Communities at Work Summit, Phoenix, Arizona.

Musca, T. (Producer), & Menéndez, R. (Director). (1988). *Stand and deliver* [Motion picture]. United States: Warner Brothers.

National Association of Head Teachers. (2015). *The NAHT school recruitment survey 2015*. London: Author. Accessed at https://www.schoolsweek.co.uk/wp-content/uploads/2015/12/NAHT-recruitment-survey-2015.pdf on September 6, 2019.

National Center for Special Education in Charter Schools. (2018). *Principles of equitable schools*. Accessed at http://www.ncsecs.org/principles-of-equitable-schools on December 10, 2018.

National Policy Board for Educational Administration. (2015). *Professional standards for educational leaders*. Accessed at http://npbea.org/wp-content/uploads/2017/06/Professional-Standards-for-Educational-Leaders_2015.pdf on May 15, 2019.

National PTA. (2016). *Resolution on homework: Quality over quantity*. Accessed at https://www.pta.org/home/advocacy/ptas-positions/Individual-PTA-Resolutions/Homework-Quality-Over-Quantity on December 11, 2018.

Nauert, R. (2015). Study finds leadership is mostly learned. *PsychCentral*. Accessed at https://psychcentral.com/news/2014/10/07/study-finds-leadership-is-mostly-learned/75870.html on November 13, 2018.

Nemo, J. (2014). What a NASA janitor can teach us about living a bigger life. *The Business Journals*. Accessed at https://www.bizjournals.com/bizjournals/how-to/growth-strategies/2014/12/what-a-nasa-janitor-can-teach-us.html on September 4, 2019.

Nitta, T., Deguchi, Y., Iwasaki, S., Kanchika, M., & Inoue, K. (2019). Depression and occupational stress in Japanese school principals and vice-principals. *Occupational Medicine*, *69*(1), 39–46.

Núñez, J. C., Suárez, N., Rosário, P., Vallejo, G., Valle, A., & Epstein, J. L. (2015). Relationships between perceived parental involvement in homework, student homework behaviors, and academic achievement: Differences among elementary, junior high, and high school students. *Metacognition and Learning*, *10*(3), 375–406.

Parikh, A. K., Matsumori, J. A., Wang, S., Boyd, D. S., Dobbins, R. D., Sweeney, L. E., et al. (2017). *U.S. public finance charter schools: Methodology and assumptions*. Accessed at https://www.spratings.com/documents/20184/908554/USPF+Charter+School+Criteria12017/5ebab49e-5dd0-410d-8bae-66a7cec923e6 on June 9, 2019.

Patterson, K. L., & Silverman, R. M. (2014). *Schools and urban revitalization: Rethinking institutions and community development*. New York: Routledge.

Peske, H. G., & Haycock, K. (2006). *Teaching inequality: How poor and minority students are shortchanged on teacher quality: A report and recommendations by the Education Trust*. Accessed at http://eric.ed.gov/?id=ED494820 on June 6, 2018.

Pettinga, D., Angelov, A., & Bateman, D. (2019). *Marketing management for school leaders*. Lanham, MD: Rowman & Littlefield.

Reeves, D. B. (2006). *The learning leader: How to focus school improvement for better results*. Alexandria, VA: Association for Supervision and Curriculum Development.

Roelofs, K., Hagenaars, M., & Stins, J. (2010). Facing freeze: Social threat induces bodily freeze in humans. *Psychological Science, 21*(11), 1575–1581.

Ronfeldt, M., Farmer, S. O., McQueen, K., & Grissom, J. A. (2015). Teacher collaboration in instructional teams and student achievement. *American Educational Research Journal, 52*(3), 475–514.

Schmoker, M. (2011). *Focus: Elevating the essentials to radically improve student learning*. Alexandria, VA: Association for Supervision and Curriculum Development.

Schmoker, M. J., & Schmoker, M. (2001). *The results fieldbook: Practical strategies from dramatically improved schools*. Alexandria, VA: Association for Supervision and Curriculum Development.

School Leaders Network. (2014). *CHURN: The high cost of principal turnover*. Accessed at https://www.acesconnection.com/fileSendAction/fcType/0/fcOid/405780286632981504/filePointer/405780286632981536/fodoid/405780286632981531/principal_turnover_cost.pdf on May 15, 2019.

Schutz, A. C., Kerzel, D., & Suoto, D. (2014). Saccadic adaptation induced by a perceptual task. *Journal of Vision*. Accessed at https://doi.org/10.1167/14.5.4 on July 3, 2019.

Schwartz, J. (2016). Integrity: The virtue of compromise. *Palgrave Communications*. Accessed at https://www.nature.com/articles/palcomms201685 on June 14, 2019.

Snyder, T. D., de Brey, C., & Dillow, S. A. (2016). *Digest of education statistics 2015*. Accessed at https://nces.ed.gov/pubs2016/2016014.pdf on June 9, 2019.

Sugai, G., & Horner, R. H. (2019). Sustaining and scaling positive behavioral interventions and supports: Implementation drivers, outcomes, and considerations. *Exceptional Children*. Accessed at https://journals.sagepub.com/doi/abs/10.1177/0014402919855331 on October 22, 2019.

Taie, S., & Goldring, R. (2017). *Characteristics of public elementary and secondary school principals in the United States: Results from the 2015–16 National Teacher and Principal Survey first look* (NCES 2017–070). Accessed at https://nces.ed.gov/pubsearch/pubsinfo.asp?pubid=2017070 on June 10, 2018.

Taylor, H. L., & McGlynn, L. (2010). The "community as classroom initiative": The case of Futures Academy in Buffalo, NY. *Universities and Community Schools, 8*(1–2), 31–45.

Taylor, H. L., Jr., McGlynn, L., & Luter, D. G. (2013). Public schools as neighborhood anchor institutions: The choice neighborhood initiative in Buffalo, New York. In K. L. Patterson & R. M. Silverman (Eds.), *Schools and urban revitalization: Rethinking institutions and community development* (pp. 109–135). New York: Routledge.

Trosper, S. T. (2017). *Safe school building characteristics in Virginia's elementary schools: Architect and principal perspectives*. Unpublished doctoral dissertation. Virginia Polytechnic Institute and State University, Blacksburg.

U.S. Environmental Protection Agency. (2019). Lead in drinking water in schools in childcare facilities. In *Drinking water requirements for states and public water systems*. Accessed at https://www.epa.gov/dwreginfo/lead-drinking-water-schools-and-childcare-facilities on July 31, 2019.

Viadero, D. (2009). Turnover in principalship focus of research. *Education Week*. Accessed at https://www.edweek.org/ew/articles/2009/10/28/09principal_ep.h29.html on June 9, 2019.

Wagner, J. T., & Samuelsson, I. P. (2019). WASH from the START: Water, sanitation and hygiene education in preschool. *International Journal of Early Childhood, 51*(1), 5–21.

Wright, P. W. D., & Wright, P. D. (2016). *Wrightslaw: Special education law* (2nd ed.). Hartfield, VA: Harbor House Law Press.

Yerkes, R. M., & Dodson, J. D. (1908). The relation of strength of stimulus to rapidity of habit-formation. *Journal of Comparative Neurology and Psychology, 18*(5), 459–482.

Zuckerman, S. J., Wilcox, K. C., Durand, F. T., Lawson, H. A., & Schiller, K. S. (2017). Drivers for change: A study of distributed leadership and performance adaptation during policy innovation implementation. *Leadership and Policy in Schools, 17*(4), 618–646.

Index

A

academic data, 26–27
academic systems
    about, 101
    academics and engagement, 101–107
    assessment practices, 117
    case for codification and simplification, 107–113
    customization for students and communities, 117–126
    guaranteed and viable curriculum, 113–116
    instructional practices, 116–117
    summary, 126
academics and engagement
    and active engagement versus compliance, 105–107
    and chaos prevention, 102–105
achievement gap, 118
Ainsworth, L., 114
air quality inspections, 78–79
anchor institutions, 59–61
Anderson, S., 1
Angelov, A., 166
arguments and freeze strategies, 148
assessment practices, 117
asset inventory, 81–82
asset-based management, 131–135
Australian Curriculum, Assessment and Reporting Authority (ACARA), 72
authenticity measuring stick, 50
automated calls, 37

B

back-to-school packets, 36
Bambrick-Santoyo, P., 49
Bateman, D., 166
behavior/misbehavior, managing
    classroom management and, 92, 93–94
    expulsion and zero-tolerance policies and, 93, 96–97
    levels of infractions and, 92, 94–95
    process ownership and, 93, 95
    tiers of behavioral support and, 92, 94
bell schedules, 35
Beyond the Bake Sale: The Essential Guide to a Family-School Partnership (Henderson), 57
blended learning, 123–125
Buckingham, M., 111
budgets. *See also* fundraising
    about, 153
    approaches to planning and spending, 155–158
    budget boundaries, 153–155
    federal grants, 162–165
    other sources of supplemental funding, 165–167
    rough calculations, 158–162
    summary, 167
    understanding the setting and, 21–23
building maintenance, 74, 75–76
building security, 74, 77–78
buildings. *See* facilities
Burgoon, L., 8
bus schedules, 35

C

calendars, 35
Canada, G., 59
caring, level of, 47
change blindness, 68
character education programs, 87
charter schools. *See also* public schools; traditional public schools
    budgets and, 22, 23, 155
    capital campaigns and, 55
    National Center for Special Education in Charter Schools (NCSECS) and, 39
    understanding the setting and, 13, 14–15
choosing to lose, 149–150
classroom management, 92, 93–94
classroom performance data, 136
classroom-level procedures, 34, 89–92
classwork or homework, 122–123
codification
    about, 89–90
    case for codification and simplification, 107–113
codifying schoolwide norms
    about, 85
    codifying schoolwide and classroom procedures, 89–92
    establishing norms, 85–89
    keeping students on track academically, 97–98
    responding appropriately to misbehavior, 92–97
    summary, 98
Collins, J., 111
communication
    emotional intelligence and, 46
    families and, 36–37
    freeze strategies and, 147–148
    initiating hard conversations and, 140–143
community engagement
    definition of community and, 57–59
    educational relationships and, 46, 56–57
    schools as anchor institutions and, 59–61
complacency, avoiding, 67–70
compliance, active engagement versus, 105–107
confrontation, navigating stress and, 144–150
conservative budgeting, 155, 156–157
consistency, creating, 111–113
"count to ten" method, 93–94
customization for students and communities
    academic systems and, 117–118
    blended learning and, 123–125
    demographic differences and, 118–122
    guided practice and, 125–126
    homework or classwork and, 122–123

D

data
    objectivity and performance data, 135–137
    student data, 26–28, 136
days cash on hand (DCOH), 22–23, 158, 165
debt and occupancy cost guidelines, 159–160
Decker, J., 37–38
deficit assets, 131–132, 142
delegating/delegation. *See* task delegation
Democracy Collaborative, 59
demographic data, 26, 27
demographic differences and customization, 118–122
difficult situations, responding to
    and dousing fires, 143
    and initiating hard conversations, 140–143
    and navigating stress and confrontation, 144–150
dropout rate, 96
DuFour, R., 112
dynamic budgeting, 155–156

E

educational lottery, 108, 109, 110, 112
educational relationships
    about, 45–46
    community engagement, 46, 56–61
    emotional intelligence, 46–49
    fundraising and friend-raising, 46, 54–56
    relationship evaluation, 46, 49–54
    summary, 61
Educator's Guide to Schoolwide Positive Behavioral Interventions and Supports, An (Harlacher and Rodriguez), 94

Elementary and Secondary Education Act (ESEA), 162–163
emergency planning and crisis management, 81
emotional intelligence, 46–49
Empirical Economics, 2
engagement. *See* academics and engagement; community engagement
engagement strategies, 107
English learners, 38, 88–89. *See also* customization for students and communities
enrollment
    conservative budgeting and, 156–157
    dynamic budgeting and, 155–156
    enrollment marketing, 166–167
equity statements, 39–40
expectations, 34
expulsion, 93, 96–97
external community, 57, 58, 60

F

facilities. *See also* operation, manage the
    preparing for opening day and, 35, 36
    special education services and, 38–39
    understanding the setting and, 20–21
facilities management
    building security and, 74, 77–78
    janitorial services and, 74–75
    landscaping and snow services and, 74, 76–77
    maintenance and, 74, 75–76
    managed services and, 71, 73–74
faculty, 33. *See also* staff/manage your staff; teachers
faculty handbook, 33–34
failure, 19
families
    demographic differences and customization and, 118
    freeze strategies and, 147–148
    internal community and, 57–58
    population interaction chart and, 120
    preparing for opening day and, 36–37
federal grants, 162–165
fight, fix, freeze, or flight responses, 144–145
fighting, 96
fire safety inspections, 80
fires, dousing, 143
fix strategies, 145–147
food service inspections, 79–80
freeze strategies, 147–150
friend-raising, 55–56
fundraising. *See also* budgets
    capital campaigns and, 55
    drops in the bucket and, 54
    educational relationships and, 46
    midsize contributors and, 55

G

Gardner, D., 144
general education and the law, 38
Gladwell, M., 131
goals, measurable budget goals, 158–160
Goleman, D., 47–48
Good to Great and the Social Sectors (Collins), 111
guaranteed and viable curriculum, 113–116
guided practice, 125–126

H

hard conversations, 140–143
Haycock, K., 110
Henderson, A., 57
hiring, 33, 137–140
homework or classwork, 122–123

I

incarceration rate, 96
income and expenses, 160–162
Individuals with Disabilities Education Act (IDEA), 38. *See also* special education services
instructional practices, 116–117
instructional support and freeze strategies, 149
internal community, 57–58
intradepartmental communication, 36

J

janitorial services, 74–75

K

Keating, K., 7–8

L

landscaping services, 74, 76–77
leadership. *See also* difficult situations, responding to; opening day, prepare for; operation, manage the; staff/manage your staff; understand the setting
    importance of effective leadership, 1–2
    preparation for leadership, 7–9
    turnover rate and, 2–3
Leadership for Learning framework, 16–17
leadership history
    cleaning up failure, 19
    following success, 18
    opening a brand-new school, 19–20
Learning Leader, The (Reeves), 16
legal illiteracy, 37–38
Leithwood, K., 1
Lemov, D., 92
Leverage Leadership 2.0 (Bambrick-Santoyo), 49
lockers, 35
Louis, K., 1
love and logic approach, 148

M

magnet public schools, 13, 14. *See also* public schools; traditional public schools
managed delegation, 64
managed services
    facilities management and, 71, 73–78
    other service providers and, 71, 78–80
    technology and, 71–73
managing/management. *See* operation, manage the; staff/manage your staff
marketing, enrollment marketing, 166–167
Marketing Management for School Leaders (Pettinga, Angelov, and Bateman), 166
master calendar, 35
master schedule, 35
meetings, 33–34
meet-the-teacher events, 37
misbehavior. *See* behavior/misbehavior, managing
mission and vision measuring stick, 49–50
Muhammad, A., 117–118
multitiered system of supports (MTSS), 94

N

National Association of Headteachers (NAHT), 2
National Center for Special Education in Charter Schools (NCSECS), 39
National Educational Technology Plan (NETP), 71
National Parent Teacher Association (National PTA), 122
National Policy Board for Educational Administration (NPBEA), 8
norms. *See also* codifying schoolwide norms
    chaos prevention and, 102, 105
    establishing norms, 85–89

O

opening a brand-new school
    balance and the ongoing hiring process and, 139–140
    equity statements and, 39
    preparing for opening day and, 32
    understanding the setting and, 19
opening day, prepare for
    about, 31–32
    preparing families, 36–37
    preparing for special populations, 37–40
    preparing staff, 32–34
    preparing the logistics, 34–36
    summary, 40, 42
operation, manage the
    about, 63
    asset inventory, 81–82
    emergency planning and crisis management, 81
    managed services, 71–80
    summary, 82–83
    task delegation, 64–70
optimal anxiety, 69

P

Parikh, A., 22

partners/partnerships
  assessing partnerships, 52–53
  understanding the setting and, 25–26
Patterson, K., 59
performance data, 135–137
Peske, H., 110
Pettinga, D., 166
playground inspections, 80
plumbing inspections, 78–79
population interaction chart, 120
positive behavioral interventions and supports (PBIS), 94
positive norms, 87–88
principals. *See also* leadership
  challenges of becoming a principal, 3–7
  and dousing fires, 143
priority standards, 114, 115
private schools
  budgets and, 22, 23, 155
  capital campaigns and, 55
  federal grants and, 163
  predictable income and expenses and, 161
  understanding the setting and, 14, 15–16
procedures
  codifying schoolwide and classroom procedures, 89–92
  faculty handbook and, 33–34
  preparing for opening day and, 34
professional development, 34
public schools, 13, 14, 22. *See also* charter schools; magnet public schools; traditional public schools

Q
questionable assets, 132, 142

R
recruitment deficits, 2
Reeves, D., 16–17, 18
registration, 36–37
reimbursable grants, 164
relationship agility, 48
relationship evaluation, 46, 49–54
relationships. *See* educational relationships

response to intervention (RTI), 94
Rosch, D., 7–8

S
safety
  building security and, 74, 77–78
  emergency planning and crisis management and, 81
  facilities and, 20–21
  inspections and, 78–80
  traffic flow and, 35
schedules, 35
Schmoker, M., 112
school behavioral counselor, 97
schools, 59–61. *See also* charter schools; facilities; magnet public schools; private schools; traditional public schools; understand the setting
Schools and Urban Revitalization: Rethinking Institutions and Community (Patterson and Silverman), 59
schoolwide procedures, 34, 91–92
Science of Fear, The (Gardner), 144
side-by-side task delegation method, 67–68
Silverman, M., 59
snow services, 74, 77
special education services. *See also* customization for students and communities
  National Center for Special Education in Charter Schools (NCSECS) and, 39
  preparing for opening day and, 37–40
  sample special education flow chart, 41
  special population norms and, 88–89
special populations
  norms and, 88–89
  preparing for opening day and, 37–40
staff/manage your staff
  about, 129
  managing your staff as a whole, 130–140
  managing your staff as individuals, 129–130
  preparing for opening day and, 32–34
  responding to difficult situations, 140–150
  summary, 150–151
  understanding the setting and, 23–24
stakeholders, 25–26

standards, 114, 115
strategic systems, 8
stress
    avoiding complacency and, 69
    navigating stress and confrontation, 144–150
"Strong Start" technique, 92
student achievement, 8, 16, 21
student data, 26–28, 136
student-based funding, 165
summer deep cleaning, 36
summer mailings, 36
summer preparation work, 32
"support sandwich" approach, 141
supporting standards, 114
suspensions, 96

T

Taking Action (Buffum, Mattos, and Malone), 94
task delegation
    avoiding complacency and, 64, 67–70
    deciding what to delegate, 64–66
    freedom to fail and, 149
    managed services and, 70–80
    managing delegated tasks, 64, 66–67
Teach Like a Champion (Lemov), 92
teacher report day, 34
teachers. *See also* staff/manage your staff
    impact of, 110
    meet-the-teacher events and, 37
    training teachers, 24
Teaching Inequality: How Poor and Minority Students Are Shortchanged on Teacher Quality (Peske and Haycock), 110
technology
    blended learning and, 123–125
    managed services and, 71–73
theory of nine, 142–143
Tipping Point, The (Gladwell), 131
title funding, 162–163
Title I, Improving the Academic Achievement of the Disadvantaged, 163–164
Title II, Preparing, Training and Recruiting High Quality Teachers and Principals, 163
traditional public schools. *See also* charter schools; magnet public schools; public schools
    budgets and, 22, 154–155
    cash reserves and, 165
    predictable income and expenses and, 161
    understanding the setting and, 13, 14
traffic flow, 35
true assets, 133, 142
trusting relationships, 47
turnover rate, 2–3, 7, 138–139

U

understand the setting
    about, 13
    summary, 28
    what are you working with, 20–23
    what kind of leader came before you, 16–20
    what kind of school are you leading, 13–16
    whom are you working with, 23–28
Universal Designs for Learning (UDL), 39
Urban Education (DiMartino and Jessen), 166
use-it-or-lose-it spending, 155, 157–158

W

Wahlstrom, K., 1
water quality inspections, 78–79
What Makes a Leader (Goleman), 47
whole-class consequences, 93
workable assets, 132–133, 142
Wrightslaw: Special Education Law (Wright and Wright), 38

Y

Yerkes-Dodson Law, 69

Z

zero-tolerance policies, 93, 96–97

Crafting Your Message
Tammy Heflebower
Become a confident, dynamic presenter with the guidance of *Crafting Your Message*. Written by expert presenter Tammy Heflebower, this book outlines a clear process for planning and delivering highly effective presentations. More than 100 ideas and strategies help you augment your message.
BKF931

Connecting Through Leadership
Jasmine K. Kullar
The success of a school greatly depends on the ability of its leaders to communicate effectively. Rely on *Connecting Through Leadership* to help you strengthen your communication skills to inspire, motivate, and connect with every member of your school community.
BKF927

Building Your Building
Jasmine K. Kullar and Scott A. Cunningham
A growing teacher attrition rate, combined with fewer teachers entering the profession, has created a teacher shortage in many schools. In *Building Your Building*, the authors detail how school administrators can overcome these challenges to ensure they hire—and retain—great teachers.
BKF896

Finding Fulfillment
Robin Noble
Develop a renewed sense of well-being, satisfaction, and happiness in your career. Designed for teachers and administrators, *Finding Fulfillment* outlines how to develop processes and best practices that impact not only your students' growth but also your growth as an educator and change-maker.
BKF893

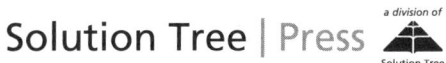

Visit SolutionTree.com or call 800.733.6786 to order.

GL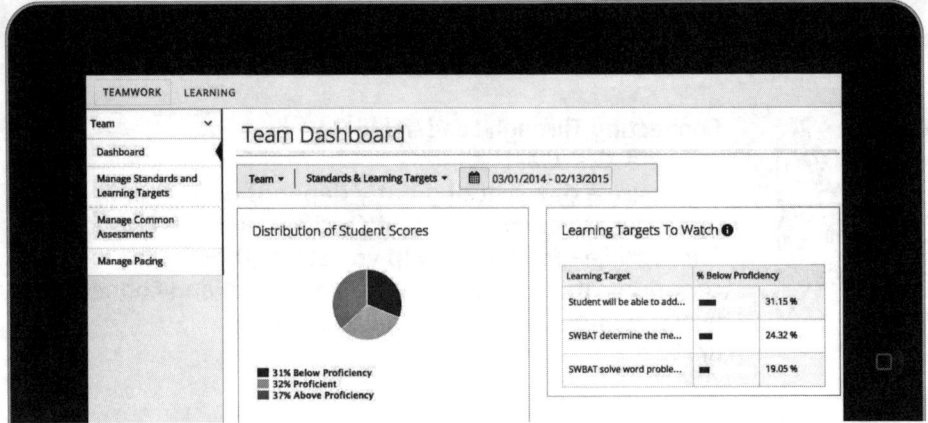BAL PD

The **Power to Improve** Is in Your Hands

Global PD gives educators focused and goals-oriented training from top experts. You can rely on this innovative online tool to improve instruction in every classroom.

- Get unlimited, on-demand access to guided video and book content from top Solution Tree authors.

- Improve practices with personalized virtual coaching from PLC-certified trainers.

- Customize learning based on skill level and time commitments.

▶ **REQUEST A FREE DEMO TODAY**
SolutionTree.com/GlobalPD